ENDANGERING
PROSPERITY

ENDANGERING PROSPERITY

A Global View of the American School

Eric A. Hanushek
Paul E. Peterson
Ludger Woessmann

BROOKINGS INSTITUTION PRESS
Washington, D.C.

Copyright © 2013
THE BROOKINGS INSTITUTION
1775 Massachusetts Avenue, N.W., Washington, D.C. 20036
www.brookings.edu

Library of Congress Cataloging-in-Publication data is available.
ISBN 978-0-8157-0373-0 (pbk. : alk. paper)

9 8 7 6 5 4 3 2 1

Printed on acid-free paper

Typeset in Sabon

Composition by Circle Graphics
Columbia, Maryland

Printed by R. R. Donnelley
Harrisonburg, Virginia

CONTENTS

CONTENTS

Figures and Table

FOREWORD

The Duke of Wellington famously remarked that the battle of Waterloo was won on the playing fields of Eton. That was in an elitist age. Today, the battle for America's future will be won or lost in its public schools. Unfortunately, victory is not at hand. Indeed, as this book's powerful indictment of the status quo points out, the battle is being lost.

The evidence of international comparison is now clear. American students lag badly and pervasively. Our students lag behind students not just in Asia, but in Europe and other parts of the Americas. It is not just disadvantaged students or a group of weak students who lag, but also American students from advantaged backgrounds. Americans are badly underrepresented among the world's highest achievers. While there are issues of measurement that warrant further examination and there are some apparent differences across subject area, the overwhelming fact of weak academic achievement among American youth can no longer be in dispute. Here is a metric for gauging education that will be more familiar to many readers than the tests on which the authors rely. I have asked a number of experts the simple question—If every American seventeen-year-old took the math and verbal SAT, what would the median scores be? The question cannot be answered with precision, because the experiment has not been done and those who in fact take the test are far from a random sample. But I am convinced on the basis of these conversations and some look at the data that the answer would surely lie in the sub-400 and perhaps the sub-350 range. That means half of our working population would perform below this threshold.

The great contribution of this book is to show how much damage is inflicted on our economy. In an agricultural economy nothing is more important than the quality of the land being farmed. In an industrial economy, nothing is more important than the quality of the business organizations involved in production. And in a knowledge economy nothing is more important than the cognitive quality of those who produce goods and services. And so education has become and likely will continue to be even more important for economic performance at the individual and the national level.

There is an additional point as well. In addition to the challenge represented by lagging overall economic performance, the United States is challenged by rising inequality. The share of income going to the top 1 percent and, even more, the top .01 percent of the population has soared over the last generation. The fraction of those who do not and perhaps cannot hold productive employment has risen sharply. Indeed, one-fifth of men between the ages of twenty-five and fifty-four are not working today, and the figure is likely to remain close to one-sixth, even when cyclical recovery is complete.

As one would expect, those at the top are disproportionately very well educated. And those struggling very much tend to lack strong educational backgrounds. So strengthening education helps. But there is a more subtle point as well. In addition to absolute productive capacity, the wage for different types of labor reflects relative scarcity as well. As we improve education and make educated workers more abundant and less educated workers more scarce, we will tend to change the pattern of wages in an egalitarian way. Our aspiration must be to create a virtuous circle in which improving education supports a more equal society, which in turn supports further education improvement.

Psychological science has confirmed what everyday experience makes manifest. The spur of competition and comparison is a powerful motivator of human and organizational behavior. It is not an accident that no one ran a four-minute mile until Roger Bannister broke the barrier, but once it was broken, many were able to follow. Demonstration that levels of achievement, which seem inconceivable to many American educators, are regularly reached in other parts of the world should and can be a powerful spur to improvement to American education. That is why this book is so important. After its message has been digested, there will still be room for debate about how best to improve American education. But there will no longer be room for debate about whether American education needs to be improved.

LAWRENCE H. SUMMERS
Charles W. Eliot University Professor
and President Emeritus of Harvard University
and former U.S. Secretary of the Treasury

ACKNOWLEDGMENTS

This volume builds on previous works of the authors, done individually and collectively. As such, many intellectual debts acknowledged elsewhere go unidentified here.

The chapters on international test comparisons are extensions of analyses previously released by the Harvard Program on Education Policy and Governance in the Taubman Center on State and Local Government, Harvard Kennedy School, in the form of three reports by Eric A. Hanushek, Paul E. Peterson, and Ludger Woessmann, "U.S. Math Performance in Global Perspective" (2010), "Globally Challenged: Are U.S. Students Ready to Compete?" (2011), and "Achievement Growth: International and U.S. State Trends in Student Achievement" (2012). Carlos X. Lastra-Anadón is a coauthor of the 2011 report. He is also coauthor of chapter 3 and provided valuable research assistance for chapter 4 of this book.

Matthew Chingos, Michael Petrilli, Grover Whitehurst, and Martin West IV provided thoughtful comments on

ACKNOWLEDGMENTS

earlier versions of this work. We thank the members of the Koret Task Force on K–12 Education at the Hoover Institution—John Chubb, Williamson Evers, Chester Finn Jr., Paul Hill, Caroline Minter Hoxby, Tom Loveless, Terry Moe, Herbert Walberg, and Grover Whitehurst—for their helpful comments on the penultimate draft. Staff assistance was provided by Ron Berry, Ashley Inman, Maura Roche, Nick Tavares, and Antonio Wendland. Kathryn Sargent Ciffolillo provided valuable editorial assistance.

The study was supported by the Kern Family Foundation, Searle Liberty Trust, Packard Humanities Institute, William and Flora Hewlett Foundation, and the Hoover Institution, Stanford University. The authors contributed equally to the study and are listed in alphabetical order.

CHAPTER ONE

AN ECONOMIC FUTURE IMPERILED

We know what it takes to compete for the jobs and
industries of our time. We need to out-innovate,
out-educate, and out-build the rest of the world.
—*Barack Obama, 2011*

Americans like to believe that their youth are truly excep-
tional. A glow of pride spreads across the land whenever
young U.S. athletes win more medals than any other nation
in the Olympics, as in Vancouver in the winter of 2010 and
in London in the summer of 2012. It is true, as the German
author of this book likes to remind his colleagues, that at
least in the most recent Winter Olympics, Germany won
more gold medals than the United States, but however you
count these things, the United States was at or near the top
of the heap. So it is not pleasant when Americans learn
that their education system does not perform at the same
world-class level as did those U.S. athletes in Vancouver.
For example, among the twenty-five nations who won at
least one medal—gold, silver, or bronze—in Vancouver

AN ECONOMIC FUTURE IMPERILED

(and also participated in the PISA international student achievement test), the United States came in eighteenth in advanced math achievement, just edging out the United Kingdom, Italy, Russia, Latvia, Croatia, and Kazakhstan.[1]

It is fashionable to attribute these results to sizable numbers of minority students, or to student home environments, or to the quality of schools in urban areas, certain states, or regions. And it is true that African American and Hispanic students perform at a lower level than do white and Asian students, that student performance in urban areas is particularly discouraging, and that some states and regions of the country have students who score at higher levels. But we show in this short book that the problems in American education are not limited to gaps in performance between white and black, Asian and Hispanic, northern states and southern ones, or even between cities and suburbs. Even when we look at the best the United States has to offer, we seldom find performances that lift the United States to the top of the world, especially in mathematics.

Nothing is more important for the long-run future of the United States than the knowledge and skills of the next generation. On this score, the United States is in trouble, because its future, as indicated by the math, science, and reading skill levels achieved by today's students, looks quite depressing compared to what is possible and what has been achieved in other countries. Realizing the country's potential is still within reach, but doing so will take more than small steps and timid actions abetted by general confusion as to whether serious policy changes are worth their political costs.

Many commentators put the problem of schools in the context of generational conflict. The retirees are pitted against the children. They are portrayed as wanting nothing more than greater Social Security and Medicare payments along with lower taxes, implying that educational spending must give way to those priorities. By this argument, as the population ages, the educational needs of children will face an uphill battle for support.

Our view is different. The battle is not young versus old but a conflict between the needs of school-age children and the interests of those adults who have agreed to educate them in our public schools. The school workforce—teachers, principals, superintendents, other administrators, and ancillary personnel—too often favors only those changes to the status quo that enhance their income or lighten their workload. They oppose changes in the organization and structure of the school system that would likely enhance the learning opportunities of those for whom they are educationally responsible. When that happens, the promise of our nation's prosperity is endangered.

The available evidence about the economic gains possible with improved schooling underscores the common interests of our young and our old. With higher economic growth, something we can expect with improved schools, we could solve the long-run fiscal problems that are adding to the debt load of state and federal governments while threatening the long-term stability of Social Security and Medicare. And we could lessen, if not eliminate, the divisive political conflicts over the size and shape of government that have overwhelmed our policymakers.

The Cacophony of Unmet Goals

Leaders have long known that education is key to the nation's prosperity and security. Immediately after the Soviet Union launched the Sputnik satellite, the U.S. Congress in 1958 passed the National Defense Education Act to ensure the "security of the Nation" through the "fullest development of the mental resources and technical skills of its young men and women."[2]

National security was no less on the minds of members of a 2012 task force that inquired into the extent to which U.S. schools were competitive with those in other countries. Sponsored by the Council on Foreign Relations, and chaired by former New York City schools chancellor Joel I. Klein and former U.S. secretary of state Condoleezza Rice, the task force warned, "Poorly educated and semi-skilled Americans cannot expect to effectively compete for jobs against fellow U.S. citizens or global peers, and are left unable to fully participate in and contribute to society."[3] They further summarized the overall problem, "*In short, America's failure to educate is affecting its national security.*"[4]

In between those dates, publicly expressed concerns about the quality of U.S. schools steadily intensified. In 1983 a government task force submitted to the Reagan administration a widely heralded report carrying the title *A Nation at Risk*.[5] In 1989 President George H. W. Bush, together with the governors of forty-nine of the fifty states, set the goal that U.S. education would be at the top of world rankings by the year 2000.[6] In 1993 President Bill Clinton urged passage of the Goals 2000: Educate America Act, "so that all Americans can reach internationally competitive standards."[7] Two years later, the legislation was enacted into law by a wide, bipartisan congressional majority. In 2006 President George W. Bush observed that "the bedrock of America's competitiveness is a well-educated and skilled work force."[8]

Despite these proclamations, the position of the American school remains problematic when viewed from an international perspective. Only 7 percent of U.S. students in 2009 performed at the advanced level in mathematics, a percentage lower than that attained by twenty-nine other countries and political jurisdictions.[9] The problem is not limited to top-performing students. In 2009 just 32 percent of eighth graders in the United States were deemed proficient in mathematics, placing the United States thirty-second when ranked with participating international jurisdictions.

Nor is the public unaware of the situation. When a cross section of the American public was asked how well the United States was doing in math, compared to other industrialized countries, the average estimate placed the United States at eighteenth, only modestly better than its actual standing.[10] Americans do not find it difficult to agree with the summary words of the Council on Foreign Relations task force report: "Overall, U.S. educational outcomes are unacceptably low."[11]

State leaders are no less aware of the challenges facing American education. Many governors—most notably, Bill Clinton of Arkansas and George W. Bush of Texas—lifted their own national profile by adopting reform policies within their states. The strategy has gone on for more than a hundred years. Charles Aycock, governor of North Carolina during the first years of the last century, is remembered as "the 'Education Governor' for his support of the public school system. . . . He felt that no lasting social reform could be accomplished without education. He supported increased salaries for teachers, longer school terms, and new school buildings."[12]

A host of Aycock successors have echoed his calls, hoping that moniker would be applied to them as well. The 1989 meeting of governors made every subsequent governor into an "education" governor. The united effort, which crossed partisan and ideological boundaries, is less surprising than it might seem, as education is one of the most costly of state government responsibilities and one that is of great concern to the general public. A gubernatorial candidate cannot succeed without making firm commitments to school improvement.

Oddly, political leaders are seldom punished for the gap between educational promises and educational outcomes. A common commitment to high achievement has, for the most part, failed to translate into broad, substantive, real-world accomplishments. The reasons for lack of gubernatorial accountability are not altogether clear. Perhaps gubernatorial terms of office are too short for voters to assess whether or not promises have been fulfilled. Perhaps the educational work-force cares mainly about policies of concern to their material

AN ECONOMIC FUTURE IMPERILED

well-being, while the public at large is poorly informed or easily distracted by other issues. What we do know is that school failures seldom generate much more than calls for renewed effort, backed by additional spending, reinforced by still more steadfast commitments to move forward. New goals leapfrog unattained past goals.

The Distraction of the Present

We do not join with those who connect the call for educational reform with current economic difficulties. A dramatically enhanced education system today would do next to nothing for next month's unemployment rate, or next quarter's growth in gross domestic product (GDP), or next year's federal and state budget deficits. Too often, facts from the immediate present are used in campaign and legislative debates to justify—or oppose—adoption of long-range educational reforms. It is quite understandable that the sluggish recovery from the 2008 recession haunts political conversations about nearly every conceivable public issue, even when the connection is remote. For some, a short-term surplus of educated workers is interpreted as evidence that young adults are too well educated, while, for others, high rates of short-term unemployment are attributed to an inadequately trained workforce.

Such rants completely miss the fundamental problem that needs to be addressed. Linking the schools of today to current unemployment levels or quarterly rates of economic growth invites erroneous comparisons and conclusions. It may be true that our economy performed at lower levels in the first decade of the twenty-first century because student achievement reached a plateau during the 1970s, but that long-run impact must be kept distinct from the impact of the recent financial crisis and economic recession. Certainly the quality of schools now is of no significance to our economy today. High school students in 2013, no matter how skilled or unskilled they might be, have nothing to do with the contemporary state of the economy. Even the skills of those schooled five to ten years ago have only marginal effects on today's economy, as they constitute but a small segment of the workforce. The recent slow-growth experience in the United States is a warning about the costs to society of economic stagnation, and it may be due in part to educational stagnation over the past half century, but fixing U.S. schools will not immediately alter the course of the current business cycle.

Consider, for example, discussions of the short-term employment prospects of highly skilled workers in the midst of the 2008 recession. Isn't it the case, the argument went, that scientists, engineers, and other highly qualified technicians are unemployed or forced to accept jobs that made inadequate use of their skills? If those with skills are unemployed, why do we need to worry about educating more of the same? That perspective takes a very static view of the U.S. economy and ignores the dynamic nature of economies in general. When a society becomes more productive, jobs open up most quickly for those who are the most skilled, and their work then creates still more jobs. That kind of dynamic interaction between skills and economic growth has long been the hallmark of U.S. success. Conversely, if a society does not supply the skills and if the pace of technological change slows, the potential demand for those skills will never become apparent.

The Long-Run Imperative

The immediate future is locked in, not capable of being altered by anything that happens in the nation's schools. The focus here is on the well-being of the citizens of the United States when our children and grandchildren are active adult members of our society. We are not writing about next year nor even the next decade. Barring some catastrophe, the United States will over the short run continue to be the world's dominant economy, and the people of the United States will continue to enjoy the fruits of that reality. The immediate future could be a little bit better or a little bit worse, depending on the actions taken now, but short of some external shock, the range of possible near-term futures is quite small.

The range of possible futures widens steadily as one peers further into the future, as that is not locked in by past decisions in the same way that the next few years are. And the long-term path depends on decisions that are now being made, either explicitly or implicitly. Unfortunately, the consequences of those decisions will not be fully known until they, too, cannot be altered.

The long-run future of the U.S. economy depends crucially on the capacities and skills of those being educated today. Those skills will have their impact when today's youth become the core of our labor force and our society. Unfortunately, we know that the United States today is not doing as well as other countries either in lifting all students up to math and reading proficiency or in bringing a significant share up to an advanced level of accomplishment. When only 7 percent of students perform at the advanced level in math and only 32 percent are deemed proficient, and when at the same time an educated workforce is key to international standing and economic growth, a long-term challenge stares a nation in the face.

Comparisons with other countries tell us what can and must be done. The United States is in the middle of the pack among developed nations in terms of the skills that demonstrably drive national economic growth. The performance of its students on international math and science exams provides a valuable metric for assessing its standing, and the U.S. record in this regard is mediocre at best. The failure to develop adequate skills, what economists call human capital, has truly profound implications for U.S. productivity growth in the next half century. And of course, the skills being developed in other countries will have their own implications for growth in productivity throughout the industrialized and developing parts of the international economy.

In simplest terms, nations that have a highly skilled labor force grow faster. This key fact has become the conventional wisdom throughout the world and is proclaimed repeatedly by political leaders. Yet in practice, this bare fact has yet to be fully appreciated, if actions, rather than words, are the measure of the seriousness with which it is truly understood. Those responsible for education policy have yet to show that they know and care that a high level of human capital induces long-run growth in productivity, which leads to greater GDP and, in turn, to improved living standards.

We are not arguing that the United States should attempt to retard the educational progress of other nations in order to promote its own citizenry. On the contrary, growth in human capital around the world will redound to the benefit of all, as countries exchange the products of their better-educated workforces. We do not live in a zero-sum world, where growth in other countries comes at the expense of the United States. The gains of other nations will not subtract from gains achieved in the United States, nor will faster growth by the United States diminish the prospects for other nations. A world with higher levels of human capital will, in the absence of war, be of great benefit to all nations. The relative growth of the different nations will, however, affect the future prestige and influence of each. It will have implications for the kinds of jobs and economy that we have and whether we exhibit technological leadership or take a more supporting role. The United States cannot afford to ignore investments in human capital in the hope that it can benefit from the accomplishments of others. If the United States takes that strategy, it will endanger the prosperity of the next generations.

AN ECONOMIC FUTURE IMPERILED

Could We Be Canada?

To show exactly how much depends on the quality of human capital in a country, we begin with a picture of the relative performance of U.S. students on an international mathematics examination known as the Program for International Student Assessment (PISA), which is administered by the Organization for Economic Cooperation and Development (OECD) and given in sixty-eight of the world's school systems.[13] PISA tests are only beginning to figure in education debates within the United States, but elsewhere in the world they have become a key measuring stick for tracking progress toward guaranteeing a vibrant economic future. The United States needs to take these tests no less seriously.

Figure 1-1 displays the percentage of fifteen-year-old students who were proficient in mathematics in 2009 in most of the leading countries of the industrialized world and in a sizable number of developing countries. As the figure shows, and as we elaborate in chapter 3, the United States trails most industrialized nations and barely beats out Greece, Spain, and Italy. Although the U.S. economy has many strengths not shared by the countries on the southern tier of the European Union, the fact remains that the United States is not building its human capital for the long run at a rate that is any better than those in some of the more problematic economies of Europe.

Other comparisons—to Singapore, Finland, Hong Kong, and Korea—show the United States education system at an even greater disadvantage. Many argue that special circumstances in all these countries make comparisons with the United States inappropriate and misleading. We do not agree. Much can be learned from looking at countries across the globe.

But even if the results from the above-mentioned nations are dismissed, it is difficult to argue that Canada is completely different from the United States. After all, the two countries share a common language, a common heritage, and a common border

AN ECONOMIC FUTURE IMPERILED

Figure 1-1. The United States in International Perspective: Proficient Students in Math, Class of 2011

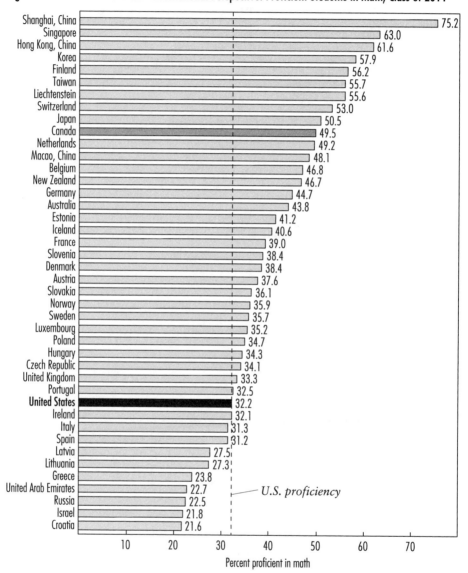

Percent proficient in math

Source: Authors' calculations.

Note: The percent proficient, calculated for countries that participated in PISA 2009, is displayed for all countries with greater than 20 percent of their students proficient in math. Countries with a smaller percentage of proficient students are, in declining order, as follows: Turkey, Serbia, Bulgaria, Uruguay, Trinidad and Tobago, Romania, Chile, Thailand, Mexico, Qatar, Kazakhstan, Argentina, Azerbaijan, Montenegro, Brazil, Albania, Jordan, Peru, Colombia, Panama, Tunisia, Indonesia, and Kyrgystan. See appendix A for methodology.

that is several thousand miles long. Canadian students go to schools just a short distance away from their U.S. counterparts. Yet on average, the students just north of the U.S. border are dramatically outpacing their U.S. peers.

The difference between U.S. and Canadian educational performance today provides a dramatic illustration of how the economic future of the United States relates to educational achievement and, ultimately, to the human capital of the country. Consider the possibility that the United States reaches the Canadian level of performance by the year 2025. Assuming that historical patterns of economic growth are an accurate guide to the future, the average annual income of every worker in the United States over the next eighty years would be 20 percent higher, all other things being equal. Discounted to the present, the gains from a faster-growing economy over the lifetime of somebody born today would amount to five times our current GDP.

As described in chapter 5, the additions to GDP from improving to the level of Canadian students would, by historical patterns, be enough to resolve the projected U.S. debt crisis.

The Vested Interests

With gains of such magnitude potentially accruing from school improvement, why are we stuck in the land of unfulfilled educational goals and flat student test performance? The simplest answer is that improving the schools is tough. Not only are the best ways to improve the system uncertain, but a sizable contingent of people would like to keep the schools largely as they exist today.

Many institutions and organizations have a stake in the status quo—teacher organizations, school districts, school administrators, schools of education—and they tend to fight against educational reforms that might alter current practices, including school accountability, school choice, and teacher policy reform.

Those who work for the schools seem more concerned about their own benefits and privileges than about the customers they are expected to serve—the children of today, on whom the prosperity of the future depends. Children themselves have little power, of course. And even their ostensible champions, today's parents, find themselves torn between acceptance of the current institutions, which hold considerable power over their children, and the promise of something better. Parent groups are notoriously weak when the countervailing centers of power are organized components of the education industry.

Is Spending More Good Enough?

Those with vested interests in the structural status quo insist that they, too, support school improvement. But the changes they propose are simple expansions of the current system: higher expenditure, smaller classes that reduce teacher workload, and added support and administrative personnel. The problem with such an agenda is that it has already proven to be an expensive failure. Current education expenditures per pupil in dollars adjusted for inflation are some two and a half times what they were in 1970.[14] An educational moon shot, as it were, has taken place. If money were the answer, the solution would be in place, and the country would already be enjoying the fruits of the reforms. But money alone, it is now clear, does not translate into higher student achievement.

Nor has another favorite proposal of those with a stake in the system as it exists—class-size reduction—proven effective. It is hard for policymakers to argue against class-size reduction because teachers, parents, students, and everyone else like the idea. For teachers, it reduces the daily effort to manage classrooms and assess student performance. For parents and students, it provides for more personalized attention. Unfortunately, it costs a lot of money. A one-third reduction in class size drives up the cost of instruction by 50 percent. At a time when fiscal pressures affect all levels of government, such increments in expenditure are simply not feasible. Even more to the point, class-size reduction in the past has not brought higher achievement. Despite a one-third drop in the pupil-teacher ratio since 1970, the performance of our seventeen-year-olds remains stagnant.[15]

A central feature of these and similar policies of the past two decades is that they do not change the basic structure and incentives of schools. They amount to an enriched status quo. We should now realize that the stakes in educational policy are enormous. Both individual livelihood and national well-being hinge on improving the outcomes of our schools. Among the many reforms that need to be introduced to make schools more effective are policies that could enhance the overall quality of the teaching force. On this topic the research is unequivocal. Highly effective teachers have an enormous impact on students, as do highly ineffective teachers, though in the opposite direction.

Those who favor the status quo would attempt to enhance the quality of the teaching force by increasing pay, or giving teachers more in-service preparation, or requiring them to earn more credentials (a master's degree, for example), or reducing the number of students in the classroom. All these steps are easily taken because they call for no change in the structure of the school system; they can all be implemented without imposing burdens on existing stakeholders, and if anything, they expand the corps of self-interested employees. The only group to suffer is the taxpayer.

But these policies, which have been proposed and implemented again and again over the past half century, have not changed a stagnant system. Instead, it has become increasingly unable to keep up with the rest of the world. Taxpayers and policymakers have consistently been willing to provide added support to schools in hopes of reaping higher achievement, and a half century of failure has only led to further calls for added resources.

Our view is that much more fundamental changes need to be made. The usual response to such suggestions is, well, it is just too hard to do these things. And it is hard, because the currently empowered adults are well organized and aggressive in opposing significant changes. But they do so at the peril of the nation.

Plan of the Book

Our objectives are not to explain the deep causes of past failures nor to detail the specific reforms that need to be undertaken. All three authors have expressed clear views in other publications on particular initiatives that might be taken. Our purpose here is to add urgency to calls for structural reform by documenting how dramatically the United States school system has failed its students and its citizens. To move forward to a different and better future, we must first understand the magnitude of the situation facing the country today.

The next chapter identifies the contribution made by the acquisition of cognitive skills in elementary and secondary school to the income of individuals and the economic prosperity of nations. Chapter 3 documents the relatively small proportion of students who are proficient in reading and, especially, math. Chapter 4 shows that the percentage of U.S. students performing at the advanced level, when viewed from a global standpoint, is shockingly low. In chapter 5, we show the potential long-term economic impact if student achievement could be lifted to levels attained by higher-performing countries.

In chapter 6, we look at the rate of achievement growth in the recent past both within the United States and around the world. The results are both worrisome and promising. Worrisome, in that achievement growth within the United States as a whole is, at best, moderate. Promising in that certain states within the United States and certain countries in various parts of the world are making striking gains, indicating that the potential for greater achievement growth is there.

In the concluding chapter, we reply to various objections to the arguments we have advanced and reflect on why, with the promise of enormous gains from improving achievement, we continue to pursue policies that offer little hope for improvement. If the latter can be overcome, the future prosperity of the United States would no longer be endangered. We conclude with a final assessment of what can be learned from taking a global view of the American school.

CHAPTER TWO

HUMAN CAPITAL AND ECONOMIC PROSPERITY

Measured against global standards, far too many
U.S. schools are failing to teach students the
academic skills and knowledge they need to
compete and succeed.
                —Independent Task Force Report on U.S.
        Education Reform and National Security, 2012

Few doubt that human capital is important to economic
prosperity. But how do we measure a nation's human capital? Is it high school completion and the amount of education attained by the citizens of a country, that is, the number
of years of schooling the average person has received? Or
is it the accumulated knowledge and skills that have been
acquired? And if it is the latter, how do we accurately measure the skills of a young person? The question is more than
academic. As the old adage goes, what gets measured gets
done. How we measure human capital will affect the policies we adopt to enhance human capital.

Traditionally, human capital development was measured by the amount of time students spent in school—the number of hours a day, the number of days a year, and the number of years logged before leaving the formal education system. In the United States, local school districts are typically given additional money for every additional day a student is in school. Not surprisingly, school districts have steadily improved their ability to measure whether or not a child attended school. They have reduced absenteeism and truancy rates, and they have encouraged students to remain in school until they graduate from high school, around age seventeen or eighteen. After measures of high school graduation rates were refined in the early years of the twenty-first century, the percentage of students graduating from high school within four years of entering ninth grade shifted upward after remaining essentially unchanged for nearly four decades.[1] What gets measured gets done.

Is It Schooling or Learning That Matters?

Those with a stake in the education industry applaud the measurement of the time students spend in school, because more employees are needed if more students are to be educated. Every additional year that a student is in school creates demand for additional time from an adult who expects to be paid for instructing that child.

Until quite recently, economists added their weight to the time measurement scale. When they measured a country's human capital, they did so by measuring the number of years the average member of the workforce had attended school or college. Information about the average number of years of schooling was easily obtained both from administrative records and surveys of students and adults. Using time spent in school as a measure of human capital, they were able to show that individuals who spent more years in school or college would be more prosperous in their economic career later in life. Further, they showed that countries where a higher percentage of the population was in school or college for a longer period of time enjoyed a higher level of economic growth. Those findings propelled further efforts to measure time in school more accurately and to encourage more people to remain in school for longer periods of time. The World Bank, for example, has encouraged developing countries, under the aegis of its Education for All initiative, to build more schools so that more young people can attend school for longer periods of time.

It takes only a modest amount of reflection to realize, however, that time spent in school means little unless one is learning something. Ideally, measures of a person's human capital, or a nation's total human capital, would be gleaned from information about what the person knows, not the amount of time spent inside a building with a particular name on it. Similarly, the human capital of a country is best estimated from information about the knowledge and skills demonstrated by its citizens, not the number of years they spent in school. Days and years spent in an educational institution are necessarily inferior indicators of human capital than a more direct measure of knowledge accumulated.

Until the 1960s direct, quantitative measures of the human capital of a nationally representative cross section of an age cohort were unavailable. Then, in 1969, the United States established the National Assessment of Educational Progress (NAEP), an assessment program jointly supported by state and federal governments, which periodically administers a series of tests in math, reading, and other subjects to a nationally representative group of students at ages nine, thirteen, and seventeen. Internationally, assessment of student performance in mathematics began with twelve countries in the mid-1960s. Today, international testing has grown to include more than a hundred countries or other political jurisdictions at one time or another. These assessments identify a common set of expected skills,

HUMAN CAPITAL AND ECONOMIC PROSPERITY

which are then tested in the local language. Both the NAEP, now known as "the nation's report card," and the assessments of the international sister organizations that produce the PISA (Program for International Student Assessment) and TIMSS (Trends in International Mathematics and Science Study) tests have made a remarkable contribution to our understanding of the cognitive skills young people across the globe have acquired, and data from these surveys loom large in the ensuing chapters of this volume.

The findings from these massive studies of student achievement have been too often either ignored or greeted with considerable suspicion. Many wonder whether human capital can be accurately measured by standardized tests and whether one can generalize about all those in an age cohort from representative samples of just a few thousand. Those in the education industry, who may have a stake in measuring time rather than performance, have been especially eager to question the new science of testing. Even today, many think human capital is better estimated by student attainment—that is, the number of years a student remains in school—rather than by measures of student achievement based on tests.

Parents know the difference, of course. If their children are in school but not learning, they typically become concerned. They know whether or not the child's daily presence at school is adding to that child's knowledge and skills. What parents know intuitively, economists are beginning to understand: it is the skill level students demonstrate at a particular age, not the number of years at school, that provides the best indicator of how they will do in life—and how well a nation will prosper.

Economists, armed with new data about skills, began describing the relationship between an individual's human capital and his or her lifetime career. Early studies that measured only the number of years of schooling showed that each year in school lifted a person's lifetime earnings, on average, by about 10 percent.[2]

More recent studies incorporating achievement measures show that students who demonstrate higher levels of achievement on standardized tests in high school will earn much more throughout their careers. If a student posts a score that is a standard deviation higher than another student's score, the first student will earn 12 percent to 20 percent more over the course of the lifetime of the two individuals, all other things being equal.[3] Moreover, it appears that the payoff of higher achievement is even greater in the United States than in other countries, perhaps because the U.S. economy places such great emphasis on workers' knowledge and skill.[4]

When students at age fifteen perform at a higher level, they are more likely to pursue their studies for a longer period of time. That accounts for one-third to one-half of the full economic return to higher levels of achievement at age fifteen.[5] This finding may be confirmation of the axiom by the Nobel Laureate James Heckman that "skills beget skills."[6] In other words, increasing skill early on plays out in further schooling and further increases in skill.

Note, however, that these differences are observed only over the long run. Early in life a person who enters the workforce straight out of high school may earn more than someone who invests in further human capital acquisition. But those early gains are likely to be eclipsed by the much higher earnings later in life of those who have enhanced their human capital. The results of individual investments in skills show up only over the full course of a worker's career.

Schooling, Learning, and National Prosperity

While career improvements for individuals are important, the impact of higher skill levels on the nation as a whole is even more significant. Students' accumulated human capital is critically important for their future livelihood, and the accumulated human capital of a generation of students is crucial to the prosperity of society as a whole. The standard econometric analysis of national income and growth historically relied on years of school attainment by the population in each country to capture the human capital, or skills, of the society. But this only crudely measures the quantity of interest. The problem is especially severe in cross-country comparisons and analyses. Why would one assume that the average student in Ghana or Peru would gain the same amount of knowledge in any year of schooling as the average student in Finland or Korea? Yet relying on a measure of years of schooling assumes exactly that.[7] Fortunately, data from international tests now allow for a more sophisticated look at the impact of human capital on economic prosperity by relying upon a direct measurement of human capital.

Research that two authors of this book have undertaken over the past decade demonstrates that these direct measures of cognitive skills, drawn from international testing in math and science, dramatically alters the assessment of the role of education and knowledge in economic development.[8] Their analysis provides clear evidence that the measured skills of a country are very closely related to growth rates. As shown in detail below, the relationship is extraordinarily strong.

The focus on growth rates may, at first blush, seem like a narrow topic and of interest mainly to economists, but it is far from inconsequential. Incomes rise with improvements in productivity, and growth rates provide an index of how productivity is improving over time. Simply put, without productivity improvements, incomes would be stagnant. But more than that, the current economic strength of the United States stems from the growth of its economy over the past century.

The analytical approach that underlies the new research into economic growth begins by combining data from international tests given over the past half century to develop a single measure of skills that can be used to index the skills of people in each country's labor force. Differences in long-run growth rates across countries are then related statistically to this index of skills and other potential influences on growth. The measure of the quality of education for the analysis summarized here is a simple average of the mathematics and science scores across international tests, interpreted as a proxy for the average educational performance of the whole labor force.[9] This measure encompasses overall cognitive skills, not just those learned in school. Thus whether skills are developed at home, in school, or elsewhere, they are implicitly included in the growth analyses.[10]

The summary relationship is depicted in figure 2-1. After controlling for the initial level of GDP per capita and for years of schooling, the test score measure reveals a strong, statistically significant effect of cognitive skills on the growth of real GDP per capita from 1960 to 2009.[11] Two things are important to note about this picture. First, the countries in the figure are quite closely grouped around the line. This suggests that there are not a lot of factors influencing growth rates other than those included in the analysis.

Second, the steepness of the line indicates a powerful impact of human capital on growth rates. Variations in math and science skills translate into dramatic differences in economic growth rates, disparities that can neither be assumed away nor ignored. Just how important skills are for economic outcomes is the subject of chapter 5. For now, we simply draw attention to the importance of achievement differences.

One other feature of this relationship is significant. Recall that economists have previously shown school attainment, the number of years of schooling, to be positively associated with growth. But as shown in figure 2-2, the relationship between years of schooling and growth is tiny and does not survive tests of statistical significance after the inclusion in the analysis of test performance, a direct measure of human capital. This fact points to the central role of knowledge and skills in economic growth. It also

Figure 2-1. What Skills Mean: Test Scores and Long-Run Economic Growth, 1960–2009

Conditional annual growth rate (percent)

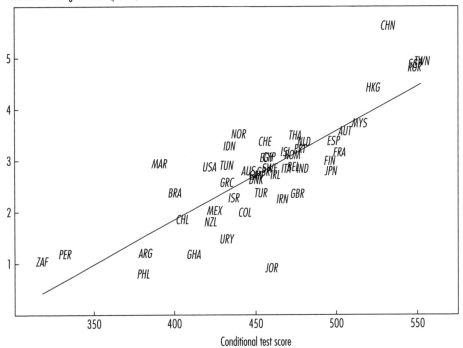

Conditional test score

Source: Authors' calculations based on Hanushek and Woessmann (2012a).
Note: This is an added-variable plot of a regression of the average annual rate of growth (in percent) of real GDP per capita in 1960–2009 on the initial level of real GDP per capita in 1960, average test scores on international student achievement tests (varying by country, 1964–2003), and average years of schooling in 1960. Mean of the unconditional variables is added to each axis. See appendix table A-1 for country codes.

confirms that school attendance is not sufficient; students must be learning at a high rate while in school.

Do Cognitive Skills Cause Growth?

But should we interpret the tight relationship between cognitive skills and economic growth as a causal one that justifies the adoption of policy actions designed to enhance the rate of learning

Figure 2-2. Years of Schooling and Long-Run Economic Growth after Adjustment for Test Scores, 1960–2009

Conditional annual growth rate (percent)

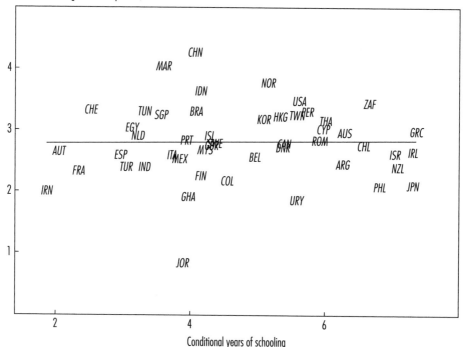

Conditional years of schooling

Source: Authors' calculations based on Hanushek and Woessmann (2012a).
Note: This is an added-variable plot of a regression of the average annual rate of growth (in percent) of real GDP per capita in 1960–2009 on the initial level of real GDP per capita in 1960, average test scores on international student achievement tests, and average years of schooling in 1960. Mean of the unconditional variables is added to each axis. See appendix table A-1 for country codes.

when a student is at school? In other words, if achievement were raised, would we really expect growth rates to go up by a commensurate amount?

Work on differences in growth among countries, while extensive over the past two decades, has been plagued by legitimate questions about whether any truly causal effects have been identified, or whether the strong correlation observed in figure 2-1 is

HUMAN CAPITAL AND ECONOMIC PROSPERITY

due to some third factor (or due, perhaps, to the potential impact of economic growth on student test performance).

Knowing that the relationship is causal, and not simply a by-product of some other factors, is very important from a policy standpoint. It is essential to be confident that, if a country manages to improve its achievement in some manner, it will see a commensurate improvement in its long-run growth rate. Said differently, if the relationship between test scores and growth rates is the reverse of what is posited here or if it simply reflects other factors that are correlated with both test scores and growth rates, a change in test scores may have little or no impact on the economy.

Early studies that focused on educational attainment found that the connection between education and growth was, indeed, mostly the reverse of what is posited here, that is, improved growth was leading to more schooling, rather than the reverse.[12] If a country gets richer, it tends to buy more of many things, including more years of schooling for its population. But there is much less reason to think that higher student achievement is caused by economic growth. For one thing, scholars have found little impact of additional education spending on achievement outcomes, so it is unlikely that the relationship comes from growth-induced resources lifting student achievement.[13] Still it remains difficult to develop conclusive tests of causality with the limited sample of countries included in our analysis.

The best course is to consider alternative explanations to determine whether one can rule out major factors that could confound the results and lead to incorrect conclusions about causal relationships. Although no one approach can address all of the important issues, a combination of approaches, if it provides support for a causal relationship between achievement and growth, offers some assurance that the issues most likely to be problematic are not affecting the results. We summarize here our investigations into the potential problems with prior estimations and their likely severity.[14]

First, the estimated relationship is little affected by including other possible determinants of economic growth. In an extensive investigation of alternative model specifications, we have elsewhere employed different measures of cognitive skills, various groupings of countries (including some that eliminate regional differences), and specific subperiods of economic growth. These efforts show a consistency in the alternative estimates, in both quantitative impacts and statistical significance, not often observed in cross-country growth modeling. Moreover, measures of geographical location, political stability, capital stock, and population growth do not significantly affect the estimated impact of cognitive skills. These specification tests minimize the likelihood that the relationship is due to some omitted factor not included in the analysis, though, of course, one still cannot exclude the possibility that some other factor has been overlooked.

Second, the most obvious reverse-causality issues arise because our analysis relates growth rates over the period 1960 to 2009 to test scores for roughly the same period. To address this directly, we separate the timing of the analysis by estimating the effect of scores on tests conducted only until 1984 on economic growth in the period since 1985. In this analysis, available for a sample of twenty-five countries, test score performance predates the period when growth takes place, making it clear that increased growth is the consequence, not the cause, of the test performance. This more precise estimation of the causal connection shows a positive effect of early test scores on growth rates that is almost twice as large as the one displayed in figure 2-1. The strengthening of the relationship may be due to the more exact measurement of the connection between test performance and subsequent growth or, possibly to the fact that human capital is becoming increasingly important for economic growth.

But if we can be quite confident that the connection between human capital and economic growth is causal (and not the reverse of what we posit), the powerful relationship displayed in figure 2-1 does not prove that school policies are the determinants of student test scores. After all, achievement may arise because of health and nutrition differences in the population or simply because of cultural differences regarding learning and testing. But it is possible to examine the impact of variations in achievement that arise directly from institutional characteristics of each country's school system (exit examinations, autonomy, relative teacher salaries, and private schooling) on growth.[15] This estimation of the growth relationship yields essentially the same results as shown in figure 2-1, lending support both to the causal interpretation of the effect of cognitive skills and to the conclusion that schooling policies can have direct economic returns.

Nonetheless, countries that have good economic institutions may have good schooling institutions, so that this approach, while guarding against simple reverse causality, does not entirely eliminate the possibility that some other factor could be affecting the relationship. In other words, a fourth concern is that countries with good economies also have good school systems, implying that those that grow faster because of the basic economic factors also have high achievement. In this case, achievement is simply a reflection of other important aspects of the economy and not the driving force in growth.

To address this issue, one can estimate the effect of differences in measured skills within a single economy, thus eliminating institutional or cultural factors that may make the economies of different countries grow faster. This can readily be done for immigrants to the United States who have been educated in their home countries and who can be compared to those immigrants educated only in the United States. Since the two groups are within the single labor market of the United States, any differences in labor market returns associated with cognitive skills cannot arise because of differences in the economy or culture of their home country. Looking at labor market returns, the cognitive skills seen in the immigrant's home country lead to higher incomes only if the immigrant was in fact educated in the home country. Immigrants from the same home country schooled in the United States see no economic return to home-country test scores, thus pinpointing the value of better schools. These results hold when Mexicans (the largest immigrant group) are excluded and when only immigrants from English-speaking countries are included. While not altogether conclusive, this comparative analysis (often called a difference-in-differences approach) rules out the possibility that test scores simply reflect cultural factors or economic institutions of the home country.[16] It also lends further support to the potential role of schools in changing the cognitive skills of citizens in economically meaningful ways.

Fifth, for those countries that have participated in testing at different points over the past half century, we can observe whether or not students seem to be getting better or worse over time. (For more recent periods, we look at changes over time in detail in chapter 6.) Building on this, perhaps the toughest test of causality is relating changes in test scores to changes in growth rates. If test score improvements actually increase growth rates, it should show up in such a relationship. This approach implicitly eliminates country-specific economic and cultural factors because it looks at what happens over time within each country. Figure 2-3 plots the magnitude of trends in educational performance and the magnitude of trends in growth rates over time for twelve OECD countries.[17] This investigation provides more evidence of the causal influence of cognitive skills (although the small number of countries is obviously problematic). The gains in test scores over time are strongly related to the gains in growth rates over time.[18] As with the other approaches, this analysis must presume that the pattern of achievement changes has been occurring over a long time, because it is not the achievement of school children but the skills of workers that count. Nonetheless, the consistency of the patterns and the similarity in magnitude of the estimates to the basic growth models are striking.

HUMAN CAPITAL AND ECONOMIC PROSPERITY

Figure 2-3. What Skills Mean: Changes in Test Scores and Changes in Annual Growth Rates

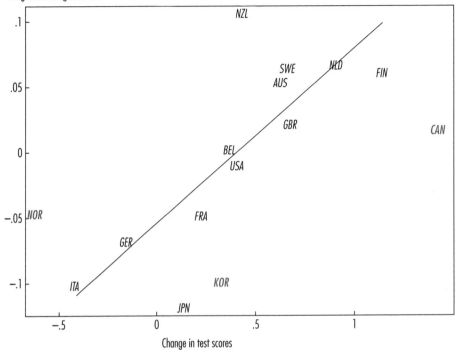

Change in annual growth rate

Change in test scores

Source: Hanushek and Woessmann (2012a).
Note: Changes in the annual growth rate of GDP per capita, 1975 to 2000. Changes in average test scores, which vary by country, 1964–2003. No test scores are available for Norway, Korea, and Canada before 1980; they are not included in calculation of regression line. See source for further methodological details. See appendix table A-1 for country codes.

Again, each approach to determining causation is subject to its own uncertainty. Nonetheless, the combined evidence consistently points to the conclusion that differences in cognitive skills lead to significant differences in economic growth. Moreover, even if issues related to omitted factors or reverse causation remain, it seems very unlikely that these cause *all* of the estimated effects.

To conclude, a wide variety of tests support the claim that the level of human capital acquired by young people while in school has a direct, causal effect on a country's economic growth rate. Further, these tests indicate that school policy, if effective in raising cognitive skills, is an important force in economic development. While other factors—culture, health, and so forth—may affect the level of cognitive skills in an economy, schools add their own contribution to the acquisition of human capital within a society. But obtaining more years of schooling, by itself, will have little effect on economic growth rates—unless that additional schooling enhances student learning. A conclusion that seems intuitively correct—additions to human capital are essential if a country's well-being is to be enhanced—is supported by a wide variety of econometric tests.

With its administration of NAEP tests as early as 1969, the United States became one of the first countries to develop good measures of the human capital of school-age young people. One might expect that better information about the extent of learning taking place in school would lead to higher levels of performance, as society makes use of the information to improve the quality of its educational system. Whether that in fact has happened is the question to which we now turn.

CHAPTER THREE

A GLOBAL VIEW OF U.S. STUDENT PROFICIENCY RATES

The educational foundations of our society are
presently being eroded by a rising tide of mediocrity
that threatens our very future.
    —*National Commission on Excellence*
    in Education, 1983

If American students are to have successful careers, and
if the country as a whole is to prosper in the decades to
come, American students must be, at a minimum, proficient in math and reading. There is much more to education
than competence in these basic subjects, but it is difficult to
imagine high levels of scientific and historical knowledge,
artistic production, or cultural awareness if students by the
time they have reached the age of fifteen are not proficient
in the tools that open the door to these domains of learning.

    In this chapter we show that a significantly smaller
percentage of U.S. students in the high school graduating
class of 2011 achieved proficiency in these basic subjects

than their counterparts in many other industrialized countries. We obtained information from the NAEP tests about U.S. students in the class of 2011, when they were in the eighth grade. Then, two years later a nationally representative sample of U.S. students (albeit different students) in this age cohort took the PISA test, which was administered throughout the world.

We give special attention to math performance because math appears to be the subject in which accomplishment in secondary school is particularly significant for both an individual's and a country's future economic well-being. Existing research, though not conclusive, indicates that math skills better predict future earnings and other economic outcomes than other skills learned in high school.[1]

There is also a technical reason for focusing on math. This subject is particularly well suited to rigorous comparisons across countries and cultures. There is a fairly clear international consensus on the math concepts and techniques that need to be mastered and on the order in which those concepts should be introduced into the curriculum. The knowledge to be gleaned remains the same regardless of the dominant language in a country. Comparing reading performance is more challenging because of structural differences in languages, and science comparisons can be faulted for a lack of consensus on the sequence of concepts that need to be mastered.

What Is Math Proficiency?

NAEP has set three benchmarks for student performance— advanced, proficient, and basic. Over the last two decades there have been improvements in math performance. Yet in 2007 when the class of 2011 took the eighth grade NAEP exams in math, the results were disappointingly low. Just 7 percent of the students were performing at or above the advanced level, only 32 percent were scoring above the proficiency bar, while 29 percent were performing below the basic level. But what do these levels mean substantively? What does it mean to say a student is proficient in mathematics?

Like beauty, proficiency is in the eye of the beholder. Oddly enough, more American students think they are proficient in math than students in any other country, while in Singapore, one of the world's math achievement leaders, students think poorly of their abilities in this subject.[2] The governing board responsible for the NAEP, in accordance with the judgment of experts in the field, defines eighth-grade proficiency in math as follows:

> Eighth graders performing at the proficient level should be able to conjecture, defend their ideas, and give supporting examples. They should understand the connections between fractions, percents, decimals, and other mathematical topics such as algebra and functions. . . . Quantity and spatial relationships in problem solving and reasoning should be familiar to them, and they should be able to convey underlying reasoning skills beyond the level of arithmetic. . . . These students should make inferences from data and graphs, apply properties of informal geometry, and accurately use the tools of technology. Students at this level should . . . be able to calculate, evaluate, and communicate results within the domain of statistics and probability.[3]

Although NAEP's definition may be too abstract to give a complete sense of what the governing board had in mind, a concrete example from the sample test that was generally answered correctly by students deemed proficient puts some flesh on the bones: "Three tennis balls are to be stacked one on top of another in a cylindrical can. The radius of each tennis ball is 3 centimeters. To the nearest whole centimeter, what should be the minimum height of the can?

Explain why you chose the height that you did. Your explanation should include a diagram." If you chose eighteen centimeters from a list of five choices, you are in the company of the 28 percent of U.S. eighth graders from the class of 2011 who answered this question correctly.[4]

The question is not a gimme. If you are proficient in eighth-grade math, then you know enough geometry to figure out that a diameter is twice the length of a radius and three balls stacked on top of one another come to eighteen centimeters.[5] On the other hand, there seems to be little need for knowledge of algebra or advanced geometry.

Only 32 percent of U.S. eighth graders were able to score well enough on this test to be declared at or above the proficiency point. But 50 percent or more of Koreans, Finns, Taiwanese, Swiss, Japanese, Canadian, and Dutch students, to say nothing of the better than 60 percent of the students in Singapore, scored at or above that level.

We know that because, even though the NAEP is administered only to U.S. students, we calculated the proficiency level for students around the globe by equating U.S. students' performance on the NAEP with their performance on the PISA. Because PISA exams do not set proficiency standards in the same way that NAEP exams do, one cannot calculate the percent proficient in the various countries of the world without building a crosswalk between equivalent scores on NAEP and PISA. Such a crosswalk is made possible by the fact that representative (but separate) samples of the high school graduating class of 2011 took both the NAEP and PISA examinations. NAEP tests were taken in 2007 when the class of 2011 was in eighth grade, and PISA tested fifteen-year-olds in 2009, most of whom were members of the class of 2011. Given that NAEP identified 32 percent of U.S. eighth-grade students as proficient in math, the PISA equivalent is estimated by calculating the minimum score reached by the top-performing 32 percent of U.S. students participating in the 2009 PISA test. Details of the technique for equating the two tests are given in appendix A.

After equating the two tests, we determined that the definition of proficiency used by NAEP is somewhere between PISA's levels 3 and 4 (out of six levels).[6] Here is what PISA says a fifteen-year-old needs to know to perform at levels 3 and 4:

At level 3 students can execute clearly described procedures, including those that require sequential decisions. They can select and apply simple problem-solving strategies. Students at this level can interpret and use representations based on different information sources and reason directly from them. They can develop short communications reporting their interpretations, results, and reasoning.

At level 4, students can work effectively with explicit models for complex concrete situations that may involve constraints or call for making assumptions. They can select and integrate different representations, including symbolic ones, linking them directly to aspects of real-world situations. Students at this level can utilize well-developed skills and reason flexibly, with some insight, in these contexts. They can construct and communicate explanations and arguments based on their interpretations, arguments, and actions.[7]

These broad, bland statements tell us little. More information is provided by a sample question PISA provides:

Mark (from Sydney, Australia) and Hans (from Berlin, Germany) often communicate with each other using "chat" on the Internet. They have to log on to the Internet at the same time to be able to chat. To find a suitable time to

A GLOBAL VIEW OF U.S. STUDENT PROFICIENCY RATES

chat, Mark looked up a chart of world times and found the following:[8]

Greenwich 12 midnight   Berlin 1 a.m.   Sydney 10 a.m.

Mark and Hans are not able to chat between 9:00 a.m. and 4:30 p.m. their local time, as they have to go to school. Also, from 11:00 p.m. until 7:00 a.m. their local time they won't be able to chat because they will be sleeping. When would be a good time for Mark and Hans to chat? The correct answer is, any time or interval of time satisfying the nine hours' time difference and taken from one of these intervals: Sydney 4:30 p.m. to 6:00 p.m. and Berlin 7:30 a.m. to 9:00 a.m.; or Sydney 7:00 a.m. to 8:00 a.m. and Berlin 10:00 p.m. to 11:00 p.m.

Obviously, the PISA question is somewhat tougher than the NAEP question, but the typical student being tested is now in tenth grade, not eighth grade. It is probably quite reasonable to say that students are proficient in math only if they can figure out from the chart that they need to add nine hours to Berlin time. Only 28 percent of American fifteen-year-olds could fully answer this question.

While the previous question did not really require any difficult math concepts, it did require a certain level of analytical skill. In any case, this is the type of question that helps build a crosswalk between PISA and NAEP.

U.S. Proficiency Rate in International Perspective

U.S. students in the class of 2011, with a 32 percent proficiency rate in math, came in thirty-second among the nations and other political jurisdictions that participated in PISA.[9] Although performance levels among the countries ranked twenty-third to thirty-first are not significantly different from that of the United States, twenty-two countries do significantly outperform the United States in the share of students reaching the proficient level in math. No less than 58 percent of Korean students and 56 percent of Finnish students performed at the proficient level. Other countries in which a majority—or near majority—of students performed at or above the proficient level include Switzerland, Japan, Canada, and the Netherlands. Many other nations had math proficiency rates well above that of the United States, including Germany (45 percent), Australia (44 percent), and France (39 percent). Figure 3-1 presents a detailed listing of the scores of all participating countries as well as the performance of individual U.S. states.

Shanghai topped the list with a 75 percent math proficiency rate, well over twice the 32 percent rate of the United States. However, Shanghai students are from a prosperous metropolitan area within China, with over three times the per capita GDP of the rest of that country, so their performance is more appropriately compared to that of students in Massachusetts and Minnesota, who are similarly favored and are the top performers among U.S. states. When this comparison is made, Shanghai still performs at a distinctly higher level. Only a little more than half (51 percent) of Massachusetts students are proficient in math, while Minnesota, the runner-up state, has a math proficiency rate of just 43 percent.[10]

Only four additional states—Vermont, North Dakota, New Jersey, and Kansas—have a math proficiency rate above 40 percent. Some of the country's largest and richest states score below the average for the United States as a whole, including New

A GLOBAL VIEW OF U.S. STUDENT PROFICIENCY RATES

Figure 3-1. U.S. States in International Perspective: Proficient Students in Math, Class of 2011

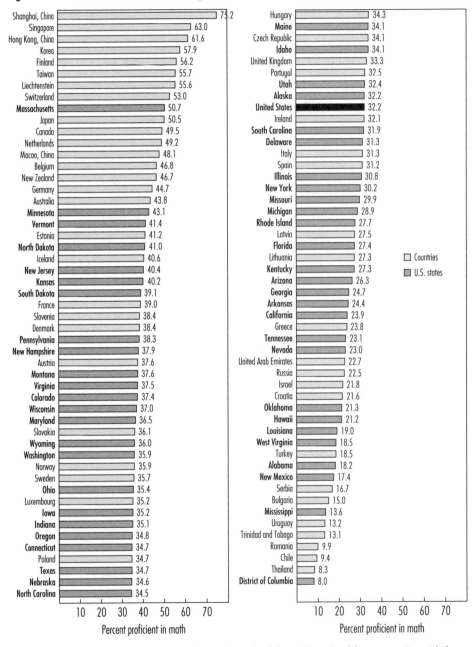

Shanghai, China	75.2
Singapore	63.0
Hong Kong, China	61.6
Korea	57.9
Finland	56.2
Taiwan	55.7
Liechtenstein	55.6
Switzerland	53.0
Massachusetts	50.7
Japan	50.5
Canada	49.5
Netherlands	49.2
Macao, China	48.1
Belgium	46.8
New Zealand	46.7
Germany	44.7
Australia	43.8
Minnesota	43.1
Vermont	41.4
Estonia	41.2
North Dakota	41.0
Iceland	40.6
New Jersey	40.4
Kansas	40.2
South Dakota	39.1
France	39.0
Slovenia	38.4
Denmark	38.4
Pennsylvania	38.3
New Hampshire	37.9
Austria	37.6
Montana	37.6
Virginia	37.5
Colorado	37.4
Wisconsin	37.0
Maryland	36.5
Slovakia	36.1
Wyoming	36.0
Washington	35.9
Norway	35.9
Sweden	35.7
Ohio	35.4
Luxembourg	35.2
Iowa	35.2
Indiana	35.1
Oregon	34.8
Connecticut	34.7
Poland	34.7
Texas	34.7
Nebraska	34.6
North Carolina	34.5

Hungary	34.3
Maine	34.1
Czech Republic	34.1
Idaho	34.1
United Kingdom	33.3
Portugal	32.5
Utah	32.4
Alaska	32.2
United States	32.2
Ireland	32.1
South Carolina	31.9
Delaware	31.3
Italy	31.3
Spain	31.2
Illinois	30.8
New York	30.2
Missouri	29.9
Michigan	28.9
Rhode Island	27.7
Latvia	27.5
Florida	27.4
Lithuania	27.3
Kentucky	27.3
Arizona	26.3
Georgia	24.7
Arkansas	24.4
California	23.9
Greece	23.8
Tennessee	23.1
Nevada	23.0
United Arab Emirates	22.7
Russia	22.5
Israel	21.8
Croatia	21.6
Oklahoma	21.3
Hawaii	21.2
Louisiana	19.0
West Virginia	18.5
Turkey	18.5
Alabama	18.2
New Mexico	17.4
Serbia	16.7
Bulgaria	15.0
Mississippi	13.6
Uruguay	13.2
Trinidad and Tobago	13.1
Romania	9.9
Chile	9.4
Thailand	8.3
District of Columbia	8.0

☐ Countries
■ U.S. states

Percent proficient in math   Percent proficient in math

Source: Authors' calculations; see appendix A for methodology. Note that fifteen countries with fewer proficient students than the District of Columbia have been omitted.

York (30 percent), Missouri (30 percent), Michigan (29 percent), Florida (27 percent), and California (24 percent).

Performance of U.S. Racial and Ethnic Groups

The percentage of U.S. students proficient in math varies considerably across students from differing racial and ethnic backgrounds. As can be seen in figure 3-2, 42 percent of white students were identified as proficient in math, but only 11 percent of African American students, 15 percent of Hispanic students, and 16 percent of Native American students were so identified. Fifty percent of students with an ethnic background from Asia and the Pacific

Figure 3-2. Who Achieves: Proficient Students by Race and Ethnicity and by Parental Education, Class of 2011

Race and ethnicity

Parental education

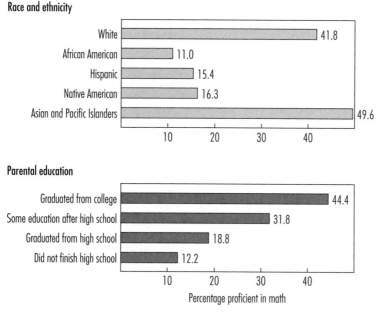

Percentage proficient in math

Source: National Assessment of Educational Progress (NAEP).

Islands, however, were proficient in math, placing them at a level comparable to students in Belgium, Canada, and Japan, although lower than that of students in Korea and Taiwan.

Given the disparate performance among students from various backgrounds, it may be worth inquiring as to whether differences between the United States and other countries are attributable to the substantial minority population in the United States. To examine that question, we compare U.S. white students to all students in other countries. We do this not because we think this is the most appropriate comparison but simply to consider the oft-expressed claim that education problems in the United States are confined to certain minority communities. This is equivalent to claiming that the overall performance of the United States in international comparisons does not take into account the fact that the United States is a much more diverse society than many of the high-performing countries.

While the 42 percent rate of math proficiency for U.S. white students is much higher than the averages for students from African American and Hispanic backgrounds, U.S. white students are still surpassed by all students in sixteen other countries. A better than 25-percentage-point gap exists between the performance of U.S. white students and the percentage of all students deemed proficient in Korea and Finland. White students in the United States trail well behind all students in countries such as Japan, Germany, Belgium, and Canada.

States vary widely in the percentage of white students who are proficient in mathematics. White students in Massachusetts outperform their peers in other states; 58 percent are at or above the proficient level in math. Maryland, New Jersey, and Texas are the other states in which a majority of white students is proficient in math. Given recent school-related political conflicts in Wisconsin, it is of interest that only 42 percent of that state's white students are proficient in math, a rate no better than the national average.

Proficiency among Students from College-Educated Families

The NAEP data allow us to isolate an elite segment of the U.S. student population, those who have at least one parent who has attended college. Given the benefits that accrue to most of those who live in better-educated families, that segment can be expected to outrank all students in other countries. It may be helpful to think of it as the upper bound of what the U.S. education system has delivered in terms of student performance. Significantly, not even among students from college-educated families can we find a majority of students crossing the proficiency bar in math (see figure 3-2). Only 44 percent of such students nationally did so. In Massachusetts 61 percent of students from college-educated families are proficient in math. Seven other states have a majority of students from college-educated families performing proficiently in math: Vermont, Minnesota, Kansas, Pennsylvania, Virginia, New Jersey, and Colorado.

The news is sobering. Some might try to comfort themselves by saying the problem is limited to students from immigrant families, or to African American students, who have suffered racial discrimination, or to others who have suffered from ethnic discrimination. But not even half of the students from college-educated families were proficient in mathematics. And children of college-educated parents in our best state (Massachusetts) still trailed *all* students in Hong Kong and Singapore.

Proficiency in Reading

The comparative standing of the United States relative to other countries is higher in reading than it is in mathematics. Even so, the United States falls short of the highest-performing countries in the world, and there is a vast disparity in reading performance from one state to another.

According to NAEP's definition of proficiency, students in eighth grade "should be able to make and support inferences about a text, connect parts of a text, and analyze text features."[11] According to PISA, fifteen-year old students, to be identified as performing at or above level 4, which is set very close to NAEP's proficient level in reading, should be "capable of difficult reading tasks, such as locating embedded information, construing meaning from nuances of languages critically evaluating a text."[12] More specific definitions and sample questions are presented in appendix B.

Only 31 percent of U.S. students in the class of 2011 were identified as proficient in reading. In Korea, by comparison, 47 percent of students are proficient in reading. Other countries that outrank the United States include Finland (46 percent), Singapore and New Zealand (42 percent), Japan and Canada (41 percent), Australia (38 percent), and Belgium (37 percent).

Within the United States, Massachusetts is again the leader, with 43 percent of eighth-grade students performing at the NAEP proficient level in reading. Shanghai students perform at a higher level, however, with 55 percent of young people proficient in reading. In the United States, Vermont is a close second to its neighbor to the south, with 42 percent proficiency. New Jersey and South Dakota come next, with 39 and 37 percent of the students proficient in reading. Students living in California (about one-eighth of the U.S. school-age population) are statistically tied with peers in Slovakia and Spain.

Looking at students from different racial and ethnic backgrounds, we find that 40 percent of white students are proficient in reading, a rate that places this segment of the U.S. population at ninth in the world. This proficiency rate does not differ significantly from that for all students in Canada, Japan, and New Zealand, but white students trail in reading, by a significant margin, all students in Korea, Finland, and Singapore. In no U.S. state is a majority of white students proficient, although Massachusetts comes close, with a 49 percent rate. The four states with the next highest levels of reading proficiency among white students are

New Jersey, Connecticut, Maryland, and Colorado. Meanwhile, 41 percent of U.S. students whose families came from Asia and the Pacific Islands were identified as proficient, but only 13 percent of African American students, 5 percent of Hispanic students, and 18 percent of Native American students were so identified.[13]

Distinguishing by parental education, we find that 42 percent of U.S. students from college-educated families in the class of 2011 are proficient in reading. In two states, a majority of these students are proficient in reading: Massachusetts, with 57 percent, and Vermont, with 53 percent. Other high-ranking states include New Jersey, Connecticut, Pennsylvania, Oregon, and Ohio.

While better than the results in math, these reading comparisons do not significantly lessen concerns about the level of human capital we are producing in U.S. students.

Schools or Society

Math performance of young people in their adolescent years is shaped by a multiplicity of factors working both within schools and outside of them. Sources of the relatively low performance of U.S. youth may lie in a lack of initiative among students themselves, anti-educational sentiments within the adolescent peer group culture, a lack of parental concern and support, distracting influences from the entertainment and mass media industries, high rates of in-migration, or even broader and deeper societal influences. Even though we suspect that one or more of these factors is at work, some of our findings point specifically to problematic elements within the nation's schools. That even relatively advantaged groups in American society—white students and those with a parent who has a college education, whom we may think less affected by these depressing factors—do not generate a high percentage of students who achieve at the proficient level in math suggests, we submit, that schools are failing to teach students effectively.

But perhaps the United States outperforms the world in training the very elite members of the next generation. After all, its top-tier universities are renowned for their teaching and research, and students from all over the world flock to their doors. Are the same percentages of highly talented math students being produced by the U.S. education system as by the systems in other industrial societies? It is to that topic we turn in chapter 4.

CHAPTER FOUR

U.S. ADVANCED PERFORMANCE IN GLOBAL PERSPECTIVE

To remain competitive in the global economy, we must . . . commit to an ambitious national agenda for education.

—*Bill Gates, 2007*

Public discourse tends to focus on the need, particularly among disadvantaged students, to reach basic levels of achievement. That focus has been evident since the passage of the federal Elementary and Secondary Education Act (ESEA) in 1965, when special attention to the needs of low performers was reinforced by concentrating federal funding on schools with high percentages of students who were economically disadvantaged. That focus continued in 2002 when the law, relabeled No Child Left Behind (NCLB), required that all students be brought up to a minimum level of proficiency.

As welcome as the focus of the federal legislation may have been, we clearly cannot neglect the need to lift more students to especially high levels of educational accomplishment. In 2006 the Science, Technology, Engineering, and Math (STEM) Education Coalition was formed to "raise awareness in Congress, the Administration, and other organizations about the critical role that STEM education plays in enabling the United States to remain the economic and technological leader of the global marketplace for the twenty-first century."[1] In the words of the National Academy of Sciences report that jump-started the coalition's formation, the nation needs to "increase" its "talent pool by improving K–12 science and mathematics education."[2] The U.S. position as the "world's innovator" almost certainly rests heavily on the talents of our most highly skilled citizenry. We think of the advanced students as the pool from which our future scientists and engineers will come.

Although some researchers say there is no shortage of technically skilled workers and expect the demand for them to decline, we think that misunderstands the dynamic and interactive nature of the American economy, which is increasingly based on innovation and entrepreneurship rather than manufacturing.[3] As Bill Gates, chairman of the Microsoft Corporation, has put it, "We must demand strong schools so that young Americans enter the workforce with the math, science and problem-solving skills they need to succeed in the knowledge economy. . . . To remain competitive in the global economy, we must . . . commit to an ambitious national agenda for education."[4]

In short, the United States cannot afford to neglect the performance of any of its students. High achievement by the most talented is no less important than raising the performance of low-achieving students, and improvements at the ends of the spectrum reinforce each other. Progress in both areas can accelerate growth in productivity.[5]

Advanced Math Performance of the Class of 2011

Unfortunately, the percentage of students in the U.S. class of 2011 who were highly accomplished is well below that of most countries with which the United States generally compares itself. No less than twenty-nine of the sixty-four other countries that participated in the PISA math test had a larger percentage of students who scored at the international equivalent of the advanced level. While just 7 percent of U.S. students performed at or above the advanced level, 44 percent of students in Shanghai and 30 percent of students in Singapore did. Figure 4-1 shows these results as well as the relative rank internationally of each U.S. state.

Several other countries also did dramatically better than the United States. At least 19 percent of students in Hong Kong, Taiwan, Korea, and Switzerland were highly accomplished. Eleven additional countries had more than 10 percent of highly accomplished students. In order of math excellence, they are Japan, Belgium, Finland, the Netherlands, New Zealand, Canada, Germany, Macao-China, Liechtenstein, Australia, and Slovenia. The remaining countries that educate to a high level of accomplishment a higher proportion of their students than the United States are Iceland, France, Slovakia, Austria, the Czech Republic, Estonia, Denmark, Sweden, Luxembourg, Poland, Hungary, and Norway.

This twenty-nine-country list includes virtually all the advanced industrialized countries of the world, most of which are members of the OECD. The only current members of the OECD that produce a smaller percentage of advanced math students than the United States are the United Kingdom, Portugal, Italy, Spain, Ireland, Turkey, Israel, Greece, Chile, and Mexico, hardly the set of countries that one would naturally think of as technological leaders.

The percentage of students scoring at the advanced level varies among the fifty states. Massachusetts, with 15 percent advanced, does better than any other state, but the percentage of class of 2011 students in our best state still trails that of nine countries. Minnesota ranked second among the fifty states; its level of performance is roughly equal to that of Australia and Slovenia.

Figure 4-1. U.S. States in International Perspective: Advanced Students in Math, Class of 2011

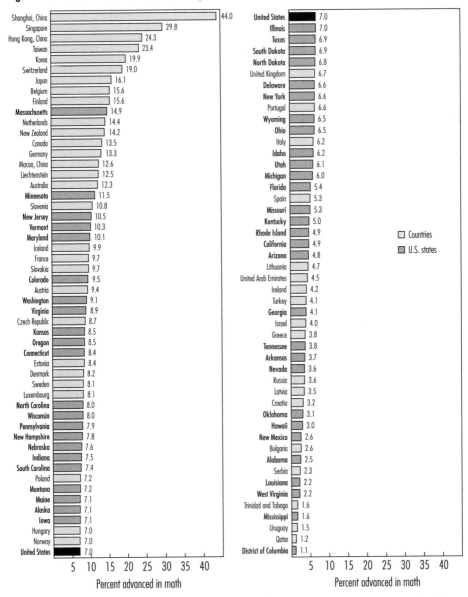

Source: Authors' calculations; see appendix A for methodology. Note that seventeen countries with lower percentages of advanced students than the District of Columbia have been omitted.

And even though California is known for its Silicon Valley, just 4.9 percent of the students in the Golden State are performing at an advanced level, a percentage roughly comparable to that of Lithuania. The lowest-ranking states—Mississippi, West Virginia, and Louisiana—have a smaller percentage of the highest-performing students than do Serbia and Trinidad and Tobago, although they edge out Kazakhstan and Azerbaijan.

In short, the percentage of high-achieving math students in the United States—and in most of its individual states—are shockingly below those of many of the world's leading industrialized nations. Results for many states are at a level equal to those of third-world countries.

Advanced Performance among Advantaged Groups

The percentage of U.S. students advanced in math varies considerably across racial and ethnic groups (figure 4-2). Without denying that the paucity of high-achieving students within minority populations is a serious issue, let us consider for a moment the performance of white students for whom the case of discrimination cannot easily be made. Among white students in the United States, only 9 percent perform at the advanced level—barely higher than the national average. In twenty-one countries, the percentage of highly accomplished students (from all ethnic backgrounds!) surpasses that in the U.S. white student population in the class of 2011. Among African American, Hispanic, and Native American students, the shares were only 0.9, 1.8, and 2.4 percent, respectively. At 17 percent, students with an ethnic background from Asia and the Pacific Islands again showed the best performance, which places them roughly at a level with Japan.

Another possibility, as suggested in the last chapter, is that schools help students reach levels of high accomplishment if parents are providing the necessary support, leading us again to

U.S. ADVANCED PERFORMANCE IN GLOBAL PERSPECTIVE

Figure 4-2. Who Achieves: Advanced Students by Race and Ethnicity and by Parental Education, Class of 2011

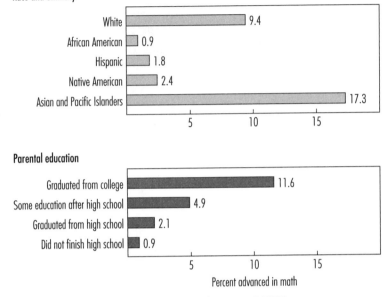

Race and ethnicity

Parental education

Percent advanced in math

Source: National Assessment of Educational Progress (NAEP).

explore performance of students who reported that at least one parent had graduated from college. Approximately 45 percent of all U.S. students reported that at least one parent had a college degree.[6]

When we compared these U.S. students from highly educated families to all students in other countries, without regard to their parents' education, we expected to find that the United States would place among the world leaders. But as can be seen in figure 4-2, among those students in the class of 2011 with a parent who had graduated from college, the percentage performing at the advanced level is just 11.6 percent. Students in sixteen countries, no matter their parents' educational attainment, outrank this more-advantaged segment of the U.S. population.

Did No Child Left Behind Shift the Focus away from the Best and the Brightest?

No Child Left Behind focuses attention on the educational needs of low-performing students.[7] The law mandates that every student be brought up to the level a state deems proficient, a standard that most states set well below the NAEP standard of full proficiency, to say nothing of the advanced level that is the focus of this chapter.[8]

In order to comply with the federal law, some assert, schools are concentrating all available resources on the educationally deprived, leaving advanced students to fend for themselves. If so, then we should see a decline in the percentage of students performing at NAEP's advanced level subsequent to the passage of the 2002 federal law. In mathematics, however, the opposite has happened. The percentage performing at the advanced level was only 3.7 percent in 1996 and 4.7 percent in 2000. The percentage performing at that level subsequently climbed to 8.3 percent by 2011 (figure 4-3). If one assumes that NCLB did not have an impact on schools until after 2003, the relevant increment in the percentage advanced is from 5.4 percent in that year to 8.3 percent in 2011.[9]

Perhaps NCLB's passage in 2002 dampened the prior rate of growth in the achievement of high-performing students. To ascertain whether that was the case, we compared the rate of change in NAEP math scores of the top 10 percent of all eighth graders before and after NCLB. Between 1992 and 2003 the scores of the students at the 90th percentile rose from 315 to 323, an increment of 8 points, or a growth rate of 0.71 points a year. Between 2003 and 2011, the shift upwards for the 90th percentile was another 7 points, or a change of 0.85 points a year.[10]

These findings are consistent with work by Thomas Dee and Brian Jacob, who have undertaken a more complex analysis of the impact of NCLB on NAEP scores.[11] In addition to estimating

U.S. ADVANCED PERFORMANCE IN GLOBAL PERSPECTIVE

Figure 4-3. Who Achieves: Advanced Students and Below Basic Students, Eighth-Grade Math, 1996–2011

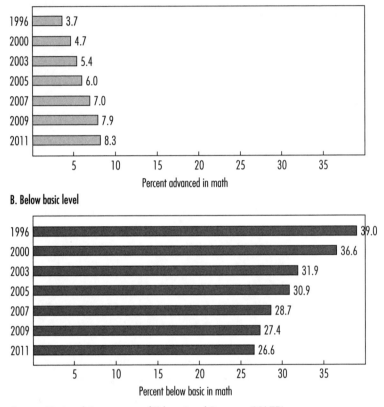

A. Advanced level

Percent advanced in math

B. Below basic level

Percent below basic in math

Source: National Assessment of Educational Progress (NAEP).

impacts on average performance across states, they estimate impacts on both very high-achieving and very low-achieving students. Their study indicates that NCLB had positive impacts on the math performance of high-achieving students, even though larger impacts were observed for those at the bottom of the distribution.[12]

In short, the incapacity of American schools to bring students up to the highest level of accomplishment in mathematics is much more deeply rooted than anything induced by recent federal legislation.

The Optimistic View from Prior Studies

Our findings in chapters 3 and 4 differ from two reports issued by Gary Phillips of the American Institutes of Research, who compares average math scores of eighth-grade students in each of the fifty states with average math scores of eighth-grade students in other countries.[13] Phillips relies on information from NAEP and from Trends in International Mathematics and Science Study (TIMSS). His 2007 report uses achievement on TIMSS 2003; his 2009 report, achievement on TIMSS 2007. Phillips's analysis compares average student achievement across countries, not the percentage of students performing at the proficient or advanced level, which is the focus here. Phillips's findings are distinctly more favorable to the United States than those shown by our analyses. While our study places the United States thirty-second in math proficiency and thirtieth in number of students at the advanced level, Phillips finds U.S. students, on average, to be performing better than all but eight countries.

The opening sentences of the summary of his 2007 report draw quite buoyant conclusions: "This report provides international benchmarks to help states see how students are doing in math within an international context. Good News—Most states are performing as well [as] or better than most foreign countries. Bad News—The highest achieving states within the United States are still significantly below the highest achieving countries."[14] Why do two studies that seem to be employing methodologies generally similar to ours produce such strikingly different results?

The answer to that puzzle is actually quite simple and has little to do with the fact that Phillips compares average student

U.S. ADVANCED PERFORMANCE IN GLOBAL PERSPECTIVE

performance while our study focuses on the percentage of students who are proficient and advanced. The key difference is that the set of countries to which we compare the United States is noticeably different from the set of countries included in the Phillips comparisons. Many OECD countries, including those that had a high percentage of proficient and advanced students, participated in PISA 2009 (upon which our analysis is based) but did not participate in either TIMSS 2003 or TIMSS 2007 (the two surveys included in the Phillips studies). As a report by the U.S. National Center for Education Statistics explains, "Differences in the set of countries that participate in an assessment can affect how well the United States appears to do internationally when results are released."[15]

Put starkly, if one drops from a survey such countries as Canada, Denmark, Finland, France, Germany, and New Zealand and includes instead such countries as Bulgaria, Botswana, Ghana, Iran, and Lebanon, the average international performance will drop, and the United States will look better relative to the countries with which it is being compared.[16]

Our comparisons of U.S. performance with that of other countries make it clear that there is much room for improvement in our scores. Were the United States to bring student achievement up to the levels attained by other industrialized countries, the impact on U.S. economic prosperity would in the long run be much larger than is generally realized. That is the subject of chapter 5.

CHAPTER FIVE

ECONOMIC BENEFITS OF HIGHER PERFORMANCE

America's government-spending addiction and its
lackluster system of public education are the two greatest
impediments to achieving the country's potential.
—*Jeb Bush, 2013*

That the system of education in the United States is lackluster is indicated by the following four facts established in
the previous chapters of this volume:

—The acquisition of basic skills in reading and especially in mathematics in elementary and secondary school
enhances a student's long-term economic prospects.

—A country that educates students to higher levels of
achievement enjoys higher levels of economic productivity
and more rapid rates of economic growth.

—The United States is not providing an educational setting in which as large a percentage of students are reaching proficiency in math as thirty-one other countries in the
industrialized world.

ECONOMIC BENEFITS OF HIGHER PERFORMANCE

—Nor is the United States bringing as large a percentage of its students to the advanced level as twenty-nine other countries in the industrialized world.

In this chapter we show that the effects of that lackluster system of education are more costly than the more politically salient deficit crisis to which Jeb Bush refers. We do so by identifying the magnitude of the benefits to the citizens of the United States that could accrue over the lifetime of those born today, were it to set in place policies that would bring its schools up to a world-class level.

Of course, schools per se are not the only influence on the acquisition of cognitive skills by the next generation. How much students learn is also affected by the care with which families raise their children as well as a variety of other factors, such as school peers, the noneducation social services available to those with disabilities and health problems, and the impacts of neighborhoods on motivation. But society generally does not intervene in what goes on in the family. It is the education system that has the primary public responsibility for facilitating the acquisition of knowledge and skills, and the best evidence available suggests that school quality is more important than any single factor other than the strength and well-being of the family within which a child is raised. And it is through the public education system that policymakers have the best chance of shifting the achievement levels of the next generation upward.

The findings reported in this chapter, however, do not depend on exactly where and how gains in achievement are realized. If the educational capacities of U.S. families could be altered so that achievement levels were lifted to world-class levels, that too would yield the benefits shown below. It is only because schools are the primary public vehicle for enhancing student knowledge and skill that our discussion focuses on how improved schools can alter the chances of economic prosperity throughout the twenty-first century.

Simulating the Effects of Education Reforms on Future GDP

Our analysis starts from the patterns of growth discussed in chapter 2, which indicate the long-run impact of having a labor force with varying skills as measured by mathematics and science scores. When using those estimates to project the economic impact of improved skills in the future, though, we have to take into account the fact that an education reform enacted today does not immediately change the skills of the labor force.

For three reasons, an improved education system will have only a long-term, not an immediate, impact on economy growth. First, reforms that boost student achievement take time to implement and to have an impact on student performance. Second, the economic impact of improved skills will not be realized until the students with greater skills move into the labor force. Third, the economy will respond over time as new technologies are developed and implemented, making use of the newly acquired higher skills.

In order to capture all three elements, we conduct a simple simulation.[1] The underlying assumption, consistent with historical evidence, is that a more skilled labor force leads to higher long-run economic growth through the regular generation of new ideas and production processes. In other words, we assume that the economy in the future will respond in a fashion similar to the patterns observed over the last half century.

Moving the workforce from one level of quality to another depends on the shares of workers with different skills. With school improvements, students enter a labor force in which older workers have less skill. To capture this idea, we assume that the impact of skills on GDP at any point in time will be proportional to the average skill level of workers in the economy.[2] Thus even after an education reform is fully implemented, it takes some forty years until the full labor force is at the new skill level.

The dynamic nature of reform effects on the economy implies that the benefits to the economy from any improvement continue

ECONOMIC BENEFITS OF HIGHER PERFORMANCE

to evolve after the reform is completed. Perhaps the simplest way to see the impact of any improvement in cognitive skills is to trace out the increased GDP per capita that would be expected at any point in the future. For example, it is possible to say what percentage increase in GDP per capita would be expected in 2050, given a specific change in skills that took place starting in 2013. The estimate is based on the studies discussed in chapter 2, which show the marginal changes in growth rates that can be expected from the acquisition of higher skills.

Our simulation does not assume any specific reform package but instead focuses just on the resulting change in achievement. For the purposes here, reforms are generally assumed to take twenty years to complete.[3] This might be realistic when the reform relies, for example, on upgrading the skills of teachers, by either training existing teachers or replacing them. Here we consider the economic value of three improvements obtained within twenty years, that is, by 2033. They involve moving the United States to achievement levels seen elsewhere in the world:

—Improve U.S. mathematics scores to the level of Germany or Estonia in 2009 (a 25-point improvement in PISA scores from our 2009 level).

—Bring the average U.S. student up to the level of Canada in 2009 (an improvement of 40 points on PISA).

—Bring math scores up to the level of Singapore in 2009 (an improvement of 75 PISA points).

These scenarios cover the grand goals espoused by U.S. presidents over the past quarter century, although they allow for more time to attain them (twenty years) than many political leaders say they are willing to wait. What would it mean for the U.S. economy and the well-being of U.S. citizens if one or another of those goals were actually achieved?

Figure 5-1 plots our projections of U.S. GDP per capita with and without improvements in the skills of the U.S. labor force.[4] These projections cover the expected lifetime of a child born at the

Figure 5-1. What Skills Mean: Projections of Test Improvement on U.S. GDP per Capita, 2013–93

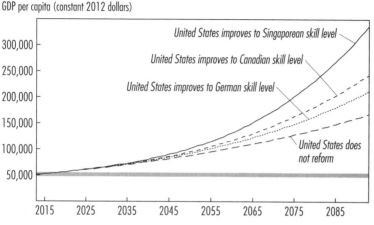

GDP per capita (constant 2012 dollars)

Source: Authors' calculations based on Hanushek and Woessmann (2011b).

beginning of the reform in 2013, which means a time horizon that ends in 2093 and that neglects any returns that accrue thereafter.[5]

The first thing to note from figure 5-1 is that society can expect to be better off even without any improvement in skills. The bottom line on the graph projects the economy in the absence of education reform; it is assumed that the economy will grow at a rate of 1.5 percent a year.[6] This growth rate translates into a significant improvement in incomes for U.S. citizens over the period.

The three upper lines display the economic consequences of improvements in skills that reach the levels of three nations: Germany, Canada, and Singapore. The impact of enhanced skill acquisition is modest at first, when reforms are just developing and when the new students are just a fraction of the workforce. Because the change in the skills of the whole labor force is only minimal, one cannot even distinguish among the lines for a number of years. But as a larger share of the workforce has acquired the additional skills, the shift upward in the growth rate from the baseline rate of change grows steadily larger.

ECONOMIC BENEFITS OF HIGHER PERFORMANCE

Simulations of policy improvements, as depicted in figure 5-1, permit calculation of two important summary statistics of the future of the U.S. economy. The first is the economic value of expected increases in GDP if skill levels remain at their current level. The second is how much larger the projected GDP with reform is compared to the total value of the economy without improvement in human capital over this period.

The Economic Value of Actually Accomplishing Policy Goals

If we want to summarize how much better the future economy is likely to be, we might add up all of the future additions to income, that is, the area between the bottom curve and any one of the upper curves in figure 5-1. But this would not be right, because the economic benefits accrue at varying times into the future. More immediate benefits are both more valuable and more certain than those far in the future. Thus we do not want simply to add up the future income. Instead, we convert the entire stream into a present discounted value, which is the current dollar amount equivalent to the future stream of returns calculated from the growth model. If we had that amount of funds and invested it today, it would be possible to reproduce the future stream of economic benefits from the principal amount and the investment returns. We follow precedents in the literature to use a discount rate of 3 percent for our projections, making a dollar in the future less valued than a dollar today.[7] For example, a dollar in 2053 would be worth only thirty-one cents today.

The range of policy projections in figure 5-1 match various policy goals of the past with one notable difference: we presume that the policy goals are reached. As can be seen in the figure, the long-term economic gains that could be achieved from realizing even the most modest of these goals are stunning. Reaching Germany's performance level would lift the GDP per capita in 2093 to 25 percent above what would obtain if no gains in student performance were realized. Put differently, this goal has a present value of $46 trillion. This is close to three times the current level of U.S. GDP, which is approximately $16 trillion in 2013. In terms of individual workers, it amounts to an average increase in every worker's income of 12 percent every year for the next eighty years.[8]

An alternative perspective on the magnitude of these potential gains comes from comparisons with the economic impacts of the 2008 recession, which has been labeled as the most significant downturn since the Great Depression. The Congressional Budget Office places the lost economic output between 2008 and the end of 2012 at somewhat less than $4 trillion, or less than one-tenth the impact of bringing our achievement up to Germany's.[9] It is not that the short-run business cycles aren't real. It is that exclusive focus on the short run has extraordinary costs as longer-run opportunities are delayed and lost.

If the United States could meet the more challenging objectives enumerated at the beginning of this chapter—that is, educating students to higher levels of achievement overall, and especially in math—the benefits would be massive. Matching the level of achievement of our northern neighbor, Canada, would be the equivalent of adding 20 percent to the paycheck of every worker for every year of work. This totals to $77 trillion, some five times our current GDP.

Think of the resistance to Singapore math that has been seen in some schools, where parents have sought to introduce that country's math curriculum. Yet reaching the achievement level of Singapore would, according to historical patterns, produce a present value of economic gains of $160 trillion, about ten times our current GDP. Spread across the future and across the paychecks of all workers, this would be the equivalent of a 43 percent salary increase for the average worker.

These projections are difficult to fathom because they are so large. But these goals are in principle no more incredible than the impact on society of the extraordinary inventions and innovations that have occurred within our lifetimes. Semiconductors, a post–World War II development, now govern everything from communication technology to automobile engineering. Although the Internet is little more than thirty years old, it has a pervasive influence on modern life. Just in the last five years, occupations have appeared, like blogger, social media consultant, and cloud architect, occupations that our grandparents would think bizarre.

These changes are simply the outward manifestations of the dynamics of modern economies. In 2007 GDP per capita was about $44,000, nearly three and one-half times larger than the GDP per capita in 1950 of $13,000. (Both are adjusted to constant 2005 dollars, so this is not inflation but real improvements in living standards.) To workers in 1950, the prospect that their grandchildren would be earning more than three times their salary must have seemed incredible.

This summary of how things have changed also underscores another important observation. The growth rate for the United States over this period was 2.1 percent, a rate roughly the same as we project for the future if U.S. human capital reaches the level now obtained in Germany (figure 5-1). Without that kind of improvement in human capital, we can no longer expect to grow at the rate enjoyed in the latter half of the twentieth century. Continuing progress at the same pace as seen since World War II will require improvements in our schools.

What If No Child Were Left Behind?

Prior projections all involve bringing the average score of U.S. students up to the averages seen in other countries. There are many ways to bring that average up, but one explicit policy that is worth considering focuses on lower levels of achievement, akin to No Child Left Behind. This policy has been derided by educators in part because of its concentration on minimal performance levels, but it is useful to see what accomplishing its goals might mean for the U.S. economy.

We investigate a stylized version of NCLB that considers a national minimum achievement level. In practice NCLB allowed each state to choose its own level of "proficiency" for its students and to make sure that all students reached that goal by 2013.[10] States chose a wide range of proficiency goals and have altered these over time.[11] The policy we assume here would ensure that all students meet some minimal performance level and that the entire achievement change comes from bringing up the bottom.

To put this stylized NCLB comparison into international perspective comparable to the prior ones, we consider a policy that would bring all U.S. students within one standard deviation of the OECD average on PISA mathematics over the next twenty years. This change is equivalent to ensuring that our lowest-achieving students were at least at the 16th percentile of the OECD student distribution.[12] Currently, approximately one-fifth of U.S. students fall below this level. In many ways, this goal is lax, as only a few states set their proficiency target below this level.[13]

The value to the United States of achieving this version of NCLB in 2033 (instead of the considerably higher objective stated in the law for the year 2013) is a staggering $91 trillion in present value terms, an amount almost six times our current GDP. Ensuring that all students are minimally proficient (measured in this international way) would mean a 12 percent boost on average in the GDP of the United States over what we can expect absent educational improvements.

There are many ways of achieving this improved performance, while also achieving other policy goals. For example, if we could bring the achievement of both Hispanic and black students up to that of white students within the next two decades and maintain those levels, aggregate achievement would rise to somewhat above that of Germany today, worth by our previous calculations approximately $50 trillion over eighty years.

While emphasizing minimal performance, history indicates that these stunning results need not come at the expense of other students. As we show in the last chapter and develop further in the next, states that have lifted the scores of low-performing students have witnessed gains among higher-performing students as well. Indeed, there is no evidence whatsoever that the NCLB accountability initiative, which lifted the performance of low-achieving students, had perverse effects on higher-performing ones.

The message is simple: We can bring gains to our economy in a variety of ways *as long as we ensure that our achievement goals are met*. As outlined in the first chapter, we have promulgated and subsequently failed to achieve numerous worthy goals. These calculations are all based on achieving goals.

Future Uncertainty

Of course, any projection that estimates trends over an eighty-year period is subject to considerable uncertainty. It must be assumed that the connection between skill acquisition and economic growth over the past half century is both accurately estimated and will hold in the future. It is further assumed that no additional major factor, other than the initial GDP level, affects economic growth. Since these assumptions are subject to error, the future cannot be known precisely. But the point here is not whether the growth rate is exactly as estimated but that the accumulated benefits of a growth rate that is anywhere proximate to what has been estimated are extraordinarily large. Even growth rates half the size of what has been estimated justify urgent calls for reform of our education system.

But are gains in student achievement even feasible? Are achievement levels so locked in by the past that gains in improvement will be modest, at best? Are the qualities of a country's education system so deeply embedded in its culture and its operations that proposals to alter rates of achievement growth are sheer flights of fancy? Hasn't the failure of repeated calls for reform in the past proven beyond all doubt that U.S. schools are almost perfectly immutable, inevitably what they are, and quite beyond the scope of any policy initiative?

The answer to these questions is, as we see in the next chapter, quite otherwise.

CHAPTER SIX

A GLOBAL VIEW OF GROWTH IN U.S. ACHIEVEMENT

This legislation [Goals 2000] strives to support states, local communities, schools, business and industry, and labor in reinventing our education system so that all Americans can reach internationally competitive standards.

—*Bill Clinton, 1993*

At this point, two questions emerge: Is it possible to boost national levels of student achievement? Are there signs the United States is beginning to do better?

If one takes a long, historical perspective, the answer to the first query is obviously in the affirmative. Nations across the globe, particularly as they transition to modern industrial societies, have enhanced the human capital of their citizens throughout the past two centuries. But perhaps long strides forward in human capital accumulation can no longer be made. Perhaps advanced societies have reached the point at which no additional gains in the

A GLOBAL VIEW OF GROWTH IN U.S. ACHIEVEMENT

performance of young adults can be expected. After all, enrollment in school through the age of fifteen has been near universal throughout the United States for many decades. There are few gains in achievement to be gleaned among young people at the age of fifteen from a quantitative increment in schooling.[1] Future gains must come from enhanced school quality or from instruction in homes, where better-educated parents transmit knowledge and skills to their children with greater effectiveness.

Still, future gains in school quality, if not school quantity, would seem likely. U.S. governments at every level have taken education-related actions that would seem to be highly promising. Federal, state, and local governments spent one-third more per pupil, in real-dollar terms, in 2009 than they had in 1990.[2] Various states began holding schools accountable for student performance in the 1990s, and the federal government made this universal when it developed a nationwide school accountability program in 2002.[3]

And by at least one measure, U.S. students in elementary school do seem to be performing considerably better than they were a couple of decades ago. Most notably, the performance of fourth-grade students on math tests administered by NAEP rose steeply between the mid-1990s and 2011. Perhaps, then, after a half century of concern and efforts, the United States may finally be taking the steps needed to catch up.

To find out whether the United States is narrowing the international education gap, this chapter provides estimates of learning gains since the mid-1990s for forty-nine countries from most of the developed and some of the developing parts of the world. We also examine the variation in gains in achievement among countries and among forty-one U.S. states (recognizing that not all states participated in NAEP testing in the 1990s). Focusing on the gains of nations and of states allows us to ascertain whether the rate of change is uniform in contemporary industrial societies or whether gains in some places significantly outstrip those elsewhere. Finally, we compare rates of gain for different age cohorts and for different assessments of student achievement to see whether the amount of gain detected is sensitive to the specific testing instrument being administered.

Three key findings emerge from this analysis:

—The United States is improving at a rate that is no greater than that of the median country among the forty-nine countries that could be surveyed.

—This may still be too rosy a portrait, as estimates of the rate of achievement growth within the United States are sensitive to the testing instrument that is used.

—Achievement growth—both among countries and among states—varies widely, suggesting that there are plenty of opportunities for schools to stimulate more achievement growth. Although current overall gains for the United States are mediocre, the potential as seen both across states and across countries is great.

Estimating Trends in Achievement

Data availability on achievement varies from one international jurisdiction to another, but for forty-nine countries enough information is available to provide estimates of change for the fourteen-year period between 1995 and 2009. For forty-one U.S. states, one can estimate the improvement trend for a nineteen-year period—from 1992 to 2011. Those time frames are extensive enough to provide a reasonable estimate of the pace at which student test score performance is improving.

Our findings come from assessments of performance in math, science, and reading of representative samples in particular political jurisdictions of students who at the time of testing were in the fourth or eighth to tenth grade or were roughly ages nine or ten or between ages thirteen or fifteen. As noted previously, the political jurisdictions may be nations, states, or other subnational units. The data come from thirty-six administrations of the NAEP and

A GLOBAL VIEW OF GROWTH IN U.S. ACHIEVEMENT

from twenty-eight administrations of three series of tests administered by international organizations—PISA, TIMSS, and PIRLS (Progress in International Reading Literacy Study).[4] Using the equating and estimation methods described in appendix A, it is possible to link states' performance on the U.S. tests to countries' performance on the international tests, because representative samples of U.S. students have taken all four series of tests.[5]

Our international results are based on these administrations of comparable math, reading, and science tests between 1995 and 2009 to jurisdictionally representative samples of students across countries. Our state-by-state results come from the administrations of math, reading, and science tests between 1992 and 2011 to representative samples of students in forty-one U.S. states.

Comparisons across Countries

The overall gains on NAEP provide the benchmark against which every state and all foreign jurisdictions are compared throughout this volume. Judging by NAEP results, the performance of U.S. students in fourth and eighth grades in math, reading, and science improved noticeably between 1995 and 2009. Using information from all administrations of NAEP tests to students in all three subjects over this time period, we observe that student achievement in the United States is estimated to have increased by 1.6 percent of a standard deviation a year, on average. Over the fourteen years, these gains equate to 22 percent of a standard deviation.

When interpreted in years of schooling, these gains are notable. On linked, or vertically aligned, measures of student performance such as NAEP, student growth between fourth and eighth grades is typically about a full standard deviation on standardized tests, or about 25 percent of a standard deviation from one grade to the next. Taking that as the benchmark, we can say that the rate of gain over the fourteen years has been just short of the equivalent of one additional year's worth of learning among students in their middle years of schooling.

Yet when compared to gains made by students in other countries, progress gains in the United States are not stellar (figure 6-1). While twenty-four countries trail the U.S. rate of improvement, another twenty-four appear to be improving at a faster rate. Nor is U.S. progress sufficiently rapid to allow it to catch up with the leaders of the industrialized world.

Students in three countries—Latvia, Chile, and Brazil—improved at an annual rate of 4 percent of a standard deviation, and students in another eight countries—Portugal, Hong Kong, Germany, Poland, Liechtenstein, Slovenia, Colombia, and Lithuania—were making gains at twice the rate of students in the United States. By the previous rule of thumb, gains made by students in these eleven countries are estimated to be at least two years' worth of learning. Another thirteen countries also appeared to be doing better than the United States, although not by such large margins.

Student performance in nine countries declined over the same fourteen-year period. Test score declines were registered in Sweden, Bulgaria, Thailand, Slovakia and the Czech Republic, Romania, Norway, Ireland, and France. The remaining fifteen countries were showing rates of improvement that were somewhat but not significantly lower than those of the United States.

In sum, the gains posted by the United States in recent years are hardly remarkable by world standards. Although the United States is not among the nine countries that were losing ground over this period of time, eleven other countries were moving forward at better than twice the pace of the United States, and all the other participating countries were changing at a rate similar enough to the United States to be within a range too close to be identified as clearly different.

A GLOBAL VIEW OF GROWTH IN U.S. ACHIEVEMENT

Figure 6-1. The United States in International Perspective: Changes in Student Achievement, 1995–2009

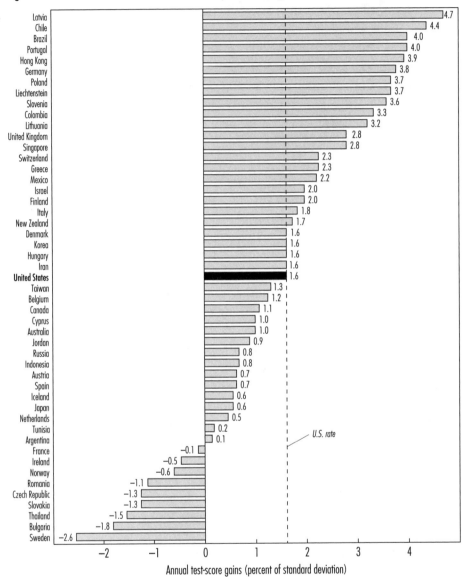

Source: Authors' calculations; see appendix A for methodology.

Comparisons among States

Progress was far from uniform across the United States. Indeed, the variation across states was about as large as the variation among the countries of the world. Maryland won the gold medal by having the steepest overall growth trend since 1992. Coming close behind, Florida won the silver medal and Delaware the bronze. The other seven states that rank among the top-ten improvers, all of which outpaced the United States as a whole, are Massachusetts, Louisiana, South Carolina, New Jersey, Kentucky, Arkansas, and Virginia. See figure 6-2 for an ordering of the forty-one states by rate of improvement.

Iowa shows the slowest rate of improvement. The other four states whose gains were clearly less than those of the United States as a whole, ranked from the bottom, are Maine, Oklahoma, Wisconsin, and Nebraska. Note, however, that because of non-participation in the early NAEP assessments, we cannot estimate an improvement trend for the 1992–2011 time period for nine states—Alaska, Illinois, Kansas, Montana, Nevada, Oregon, South Dakota, Vermont, and Washington.[6]

Cumulative growth rates vary widely. Average student gains over the nineteen-year period in Maryland, Florida, Delaware, and Massachusetts, with annual growth rates of 3.1 to 3.3 percent of a standard deviation, yielded gains of about 60 percent of a standard deviation over the entire time period, or better than two years of additional learning. Meanwhile, annual gains in the states with the weakest growth rates—Iowa, Maine, Oklahoma, and Wisconsin—varied between 0.7 percent and 1.0 percent of a standard deviation, which translate over the nineteen-year period into learning gains of one-half to three-quarters of a year. In other words, the states making the largest gains are improving at a rate two to three times the rate in states with the smallest gains.

Had all students throughout the country made the same average gains as those in the four leading states, the United

A GLOBAL VIEW OF GROWTH IN U.S. ACHIEVEMENT

Figure 6-2. U.S. States: Changes in Student Achievement, 1992–2011

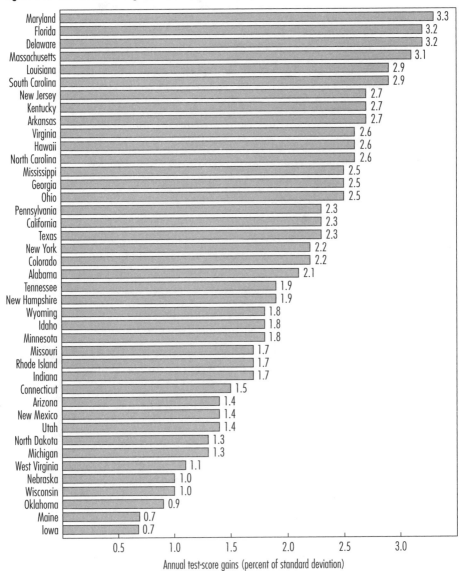

Annual test-score gains (percent of standard deviation)

Source: Authors' calculations; see appendix A for methodology.

States would have been making progress roughly comparable to the rate of improvement in Germany and the United Kingdom, bringing the United States reasonably close to the top-performing countries in the world (as long as those nations did not also improve).

Gains by Low-Performing and High-Performing Students

NAEP has set three benchmarks for student performance—advanced, proficient, and basic. According to these standards, very few U.S. students are performing at the advanced level in math, and a clear majority of students score at a level below what the NAEP governing board deems necessary to demonstrate math proficiency. A substantial majority of students do have what NAEP regards as basic mathematics knowledge. Nonetheless, in 2007, 27 percent of eighth graders scored below the basic level, while just 7 percent performed at the advanced level and only 32 percent were proficient.

It is important to understand that the NAEP definition of proficiency used here is different from the one set by each state under No Child Left Behind, the federal law passed in 2002. As mentioned previously, that law allowed each state to set its own proficiency standard, and as a result, state proficiency standards have varied widely.[7] In 2009 only one state—Massachusetts—set its proficiency standards at levels roughly equivalent to the NAEP levels of proficiency.[8] Meanwhile, fourteen states with the lowest proficiency standards set them below the NAEP basic level.

Since states set very different proficiency standards under NCLB, it is possible that they also focused their attention on different segments of the student population. Some may have concentrated on enhancing the performance of those who had not attained the NAEP basic level, while others may have focused on those close to the NAEP proficiency line.

Figure 6-3. Who Achieves: Improvements at the Basic and at the Proficient Levels, Eighth-Grade Math, 1992–2011

Percent reduction in below basic level scores

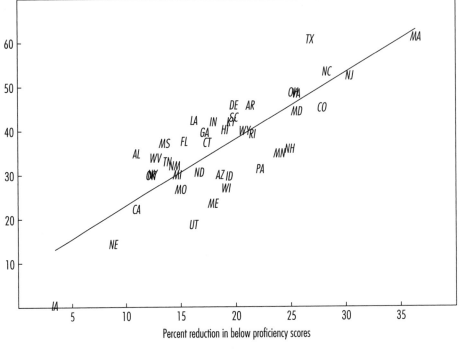

Percent reduction in below proficiency scores

Source: Hanushek, Peterson, and Woessmann (2012).

In figure 6-3 we provide a simple description of how improving at the low end (below basic on NAEP) relates to improving at higher levels (proficient on NAEP), using the example of eighth-grade math. This figure reports the success of states at reducing the percentage of students performing below the basic level on the y-axis. For example, Massachusetts went from 37.2 percent below basic in 1992 down to 14.5 percent below basic in 2011, which we identify as a 61 percent reduction in low performance. Texas gets the same percentage reduction by going from 47.3 to 18.6 percent.

We depict on the *x*-axis each state's success in lifting the percentage of nonproficient students across the proficiency bar. Again, 77.7 percent of Massachusetts' eighth graders did not make the proficient level in 1992, and this was reduced to 48.8 percent by 2011, a reduction of 35.9 percent in the proportion less than proficient.

The steep regression line in figure 6-3 (correlation = 0.81) shows that gains for higher-performing students do not in general come at the expense of the educationally disadvantaged. Those states that experience the greatest reduction in the number of students performing below the basic level also see the largest percentage shift across the NAEP proficiency bar. Yet a few states deviate from the general pattern. Texas experienced a disproportionately large reduction in the percentage of those performing below the basic level, given the percentages crossing the math proficiency line. Conversely, Utah, Nebraska, Pennsylvania, Maine, Wisconsin, and Minnesota (relative to other states) were seeing a relatively large number of students becoming proficient at the NAEP level, given the amount of reduction in below-basic performance among the educationally disadvantaged.

These states are slight exceptions to the otherwise strong correlation between improvements of high- and low-achieving students in eighth grade. The strength of that relationship is particularly meaningful, as it shows the pattern for students as they are preparing for high school. The data demonstrate rather clearly that most states, if they make gains, do so across the board—for higher- and lower-performing students alike. States can and do work at "leaving no child behind" and yet at the same time see an increment in the percentage of students rising to a level of NAEP proficiency. States in which the educationally disadvantaged are gaining the most ground are the ones in which higher-performing students are doing the same, and vice versa.

In short, what is occurring in most states is, more often than not, happening to both those who are higher performing and those who are the most challenged.

Is the South Rising Again?

Some regional concentration among the states is evident. Five of the top ten improving states were in the South, while no southern states were among the eighteen with the slowest growth. The strong showing of the South may be related to energetic political efforts to enhance school quality in that region. During the 1990s, governors of several southern states—Tennessee, North Carolina, Florida, Texas, and Arkansas—provided much of the national leadership for the school accountability effort, as there was widespread sentiment in the wake of the civil rights movement that steps had to be taken to equalize educational opportunity across racial groups. The results of our study suggest that those efforts were at least partially successful. But the showing might also be a function of the fact that the teachers' unions are much more powerful outside of the South.[9]

Meanwhile, students in Wisconsin, Michigan, Iowa, and Indiana were among those making the smallest average gains between 1992 and 2011. Once again, the larger political climate may have affected progress on the ground. Unlike in the South, the reform movement has made little headway within midwestern states, at least until very recently. Many of these states had proud education histories symbolized by internationally acclaimed land-grant universities, which have become the pride of East Lansing, Michigan; Madison, Wisconsin; Ames, Iowa; and Lafayette, Indiana. Satisfaction with past accomplishments may have dampened interest in the school reform agenda sweeping through southern, border, and some western states.

Are Gains Simply Catch-Ups?

On the one hand, growth in student performance may be easier for those political jurisdictions originally performing at a low level than for those originally performing at higher levels. Lower-performing systems may be able to copy existing approaches at lower cost than higher-performing systems can innovate. This would lead to a convergence in performance over time. On the other hand, high-performing school systems may find it relatively easy to build on their past achievements, while low-performing systems may struggle to acquire the human capital needed to improve. If that is generally the case, then the education gap among nations and among states should steadily widen over time.

Neither hypothesis seems able to predict the international test score changes that we have seen, as nations with rapid gains can be identified among both countries that had high initial scores and countries that had low ones. Latvia, Chile, and Brazil, for example, were low-ranking countries in 1995 that made rapid gains, a pattern that supports the catch-up hypothesis. But consistent with the building-on-strength hypothesis, a number of countries that advanced relatively rapidly were initially high-performing countries—Hong Kong and Germany, for example. Overall, there is no significant pattern between original performance and changes in performance across countries.

But the catch-up hypothesis may help explain part of the variation among the U.S. states. The correlation between initial performance and rate of growth is negative 0.58; states starting with lower initial scores tend to have larger gains. For example, students in Mississippi and Louisiana, originally among the lowest scoring, showed some of the most striking improvement. Meanwhile, Iowa and Maine, two of the highest-performing states in 1992, were among the laggards in subsequent years. In other words, the catch-up hypothesis partially characterizes the pattern of change within the United States, probably because the barriers to the adoption of existing technologies are much lower within a single country than across national boundaries.

The catch-up hypothesis, even if it were perfectly predictive of future growth, would not provide much in the way of policy guidance. And in fact, it explains only about one-quarter of the total state variation in achievement growth. Some states—for instance, Maryland, Massachusetts, Delaware, and Florida—show much greater improvements than would be expected from the catch-up hypothesis. By contrast, states such as Iowa, Maine, Wisconsin, and Nebraska show much less improvement than would be expected from catch-up. Closing the interstate gap does not happen automatically.

Have We Painted Too Rosy a Portrait?

We have estimated achievement gains of 1.6 percent of a standard deviation each year for the United States as a whole, or a total gain of 22 percent of a standard deviation over fourteen years, a forward movement that has lifted performance by nearly a full year's worth of learning over the entire time period. A similar rate of gain is estimated for the other forty-eight participating countries. Such a rate of improvement is plausible, given the increased wealth in the industrialized world and the higher percentages of educated parents than in prior generations.

Still, this growth—normed against student performances on NAEP in fourth and eighth grades in 2000—is disproportionately affected by fourth-grade performance, possibly leading to too much optimism. When we estimate gains only from student performance in eighth grade (on the grounds that fourth-grade gains are meaningless unless they are observed for the same cohort four years later), our results show annual gains in the United States of only 1 percent of a standard deviation annually. The relative ranking of the United States remains essentially unchanged, however, as the estimated growth rates for eighth graders in other countries is also lower than estimates that include students in fourth grade. If one tracks gains for the United States directly from PISA tests (rather than from NAEP), the estimated annual growth rate for the United States is only 0.5 percent of a standard deviation.[10]

An even darker picture emerges if one turns to the results for U.S. students at age seventeen, for whom only minimal gains can be detected over the past two decades. We have not reported the results for seventeen-year-old students because the test administered to them does not provide information on the performance of students within individual states and no international comparisons are possible for this age group. Students themselves and the United States as a whole benefit from improved performance in the early grades only if that translates into measurably higher skills at the end of schooling. The fact that none of the gains observed in earlier years translates into improved high school performance leaves one to wonder whether high schools are effectively building on the gains achieved in the earlier years of schooling.

Some scholars dismiss the results for seventeen-year-old students on the grounds that high school students do not take the test seriously. Others believe that the data indicate that the American high school is not educating the students to their full potential. Amidst these uncertainties one fact remains clear, however: the measurable gains in achievement accomplished by more recent cohorts of U.S. students are being essentially matched by the measurable overall gains by students in the other forty-eight participating countries. The United States is not closing the international achievement gap.

Interpreting the Gains

We rely on these international comparisons to indicate what is possible. The rapid gainers appear to have taken a wide variety of approaches to improving student performance. While a number of analysts have attempted to extract lessons from the international differences, we stop here and point out that the kinds of improvements we considered for the United States in chapter 5 are not out of the realm of possibility, given the reality around the world.[11]

Similarly, the kinds of gains needed to get economic results described in chapter 5 are possible if we could replicate the performance of top-performing states across the nation. The gains seen in Maryland, Florida, Delaware, and Massachusetts, if reproduced in the remaining states over the next two decades, would move achievement noticeably past Canada's current level and would bring us reasonably close to that of Singapore. It does not seem unreasonable to think that we can bring our laggard states up to the level of our striving states.

What are the obstacles that are endangering U.S. prosperity? In our concluding chapter, we turn to that question, after addressing a number of objections to the argument that we have advanced.

CHAPTER SEVEN

SUBSTANTIVE CONCERNS AND POLITICAL OBSTACLES

The enemy I fear most is complacency. We are about to be hit by the full force of global competition. If we continue to ignore the obvious task at hand while others beat us at our own game, our children and grandchildren will pay the price. We must now establish a sense of urgency.

—*Charles Vest, 2009*

U.S. schools are not helping the next generation reach its full potential. Compared to what is being accomplished by other industrialized countries, the performance of the United States, once the world's education leader, is now, especially in mathematics, below average. Nor is there much sign that the United States is gaining ground. The failure to address the country's educational malaise is extremely costly both for the next generation and for the country as a whole. Fortunately, the situation is not intractable. In some parts of the United States and some parts of the world, rapid student achievement gains are being realized. If it can happen elsewhere, including in parts of the United States, there is no reason it cannot happen throughout the country.

That is our argument. Not everyone is persuaded by it. Many are reluctant to do anything about it. In this concluding chapter, we consider some of the concerns and objections to the thesis we have developed and some of the political obstacles that must be skirted or overridden if schools are to become more effective. We then turn to the central political challenge school reformers face: the education industry resists reform and reorganization, while the public, though concerned about its schools, is lacking in information, organization, and leadership.

Possible Concerns with Our Argument

The five primary objections to our analysis are as follows:

—Standardized tests are uninformative.
—Society, not schools, needs to change.
—U.S. growth does not depend on student achievement.
—There is a problem, but the solution is more money.
—The problem is intractable.

Each point deserves a direct response.

"Standardized Tests Are Uninformative"

Designed by Lewis Terman, standardized tests in the United States were first administered to 1.7 million recruits into the armed forces in World War I to identify quickly and inexpensively individual recruits who could be easily trained for higher-level responsibilities. So successful were these early tests at identifying effective officers that Terman adapted them for civilian life to identify gifted children and place students in appropriate academic tracks. Since Terman thought intelligence was largely inherited, the idea of an immutable, native intelligence that determined one's degree of success in life soon took hold.

Out of this tradition came the Scholastic Aptitude Test (SAT), begun in 1926, which claimed to be able to identify at a fairly early age those students who could profit from a college education. It was thought that no one could study for this test, as it was designed to capture native ability, not the knowledge that had been accumulated. Only later did it become apparent that one could benefit from preparation for an SAT test just as one can benefit from preparation for any other test. Those who design the SAT no longer claim that it measures an underlying aptitude and indeed have, for that reason, substituted the acronym for the original name.

In contrast to those who developed the SAT, those who designed the NAEP and PISA, as well as tests used to meet federal accountability requirements, intend to measure knowledge and skills, not native ability or underlying aptitude. But they have one characteristic in common with Terman and his successors: the creation of an easily administered test that can yield reliable, valid information at low cost about large populations of students. Standardization means a set of questions with response categories that are fixed, allowing for rapid grading and precise comparison of performance among test takers.

The debate over standardized tests has been continuous. The psychometricians who have refined these tests claim that the questions constitute a random cross section of the knowledge and skills that students are expected to have acquired by the age for which the test is designed. Powerful analytical tools have been created to make sure that a test reliably measures competence in the domain that is being tested. Unless answers to a question correlate with responses to other questions, the item is deleted from the test. These claims have been supported by the work of sociologists and economists, who have shown that performance on

SUBSTANTIVE CONCERNS AND POLITICAL OBSTACLES

these standardized tests predicts future outcomes in life, including college completion, lifetime earnings, and other economic and social indicators of well-being.

Critics are not satisfied with these claims. They note that the correlation with future success is only moderate, as many other qualities—pluck, persistence, charm, and sociability—are also important. It is the analytical thinker who scores high on standardized tests, but the one who has insight and intuition may be the more valuable employee, the more successful entrepreneur, and the more desirable spouse. Some people "tighten up" when they take a test and do not do as well as they would under other circumstances, while others "overachieve" by focusing and responding to the competition. If a person is sick on test day, his or her performance may be far below par.

Defenders of standardized tests recognize their limitations for the evaluation of any one individual, but they claim that errors that occur at the individual level cancel one another out when results are aggregated for large groups. When tests are administered to thousands of students, aggregate results are quite precise and quite consistent from one test administration to the next. Even so, they capture only one type of knowledge and not everything that is included within the concept of human capital.

Surely, standardized tests do not tell us all that we need to know about human capital accumulation in modern society. Certain kinds of talents and abilities are not captured by math, science, or reading tests. Obviously, they do not measure artistic or musical talent or athletic talent or the ability to write creatively and imaginatively. But the question is not whether they measure everything; it is whether they are useful for measuring some important things, such as the ability to read and interpret written material, to analyze information, and to understand scientific principles. If standardized tests can tell us how well the next generation is doing at mastering those basic skills, then they are probably useful measures of the education the next generation is receiving. Standardized tests do not necessarily capture all aspects of human capital, but they at least distinguish those who have acquired the essentials from those who have not. They also correlate highly with measures of those who will continue to more advanced levels of schooling and those who will gain more from future education.

"Society, Not Schools, Needs to Change"

Although scores on standardized tests are now generally accepted as valid indicators of human capital, members of a vocal group, including many current administrators and teachers in our schools, attribute the relatively low performance of American students to the nation's high poverty rate, substantial number of immigrants, and large minority population. That poverty and family backgrounds have an influence on student achievement in today's schools is unassailable. Since the Coleman Report on schools first looked intensively at this in the mid-1960s, research has universally found that a variety of factors outside of school systematically affect achievement.[1]

Taking note of these facts, the Broader, Bolder Approach to Education, a coalition of education professors and interest group leaders, including the heads of the country's two largest teachers' unions, has launched a campaign to draw policy implications from the consensus about the importance of families.[2] In the first paragraph of its mission statement, the coalition claims that it has identified "a powerful association between social and economic disadvantage and low student achievement."

"Weakening that link," the Broader, Bolder group goes on to say, "is the fundamental challenge facing America's education policy makers." For this group, poverty and income inequality, not inadequate schools, are the fundamental problem in American education that needs to be fixed. Other possible approaches to improving student achievement—school accountability, school choice, reform of the teaching profession—are misguided, overblown, counterproductive, and even dangerous. Moreover, the energy now being wasted on attempts to enhance the country's education system should be redirected toward a campaign to redistribute income and to expand the network of social services.

Elaborating on the Broader, Bolder theme, a recent study by Martin Carnoy and Richard Rothstein argues that differences between the United States and six other developed countries disappear when adjustments are made for social class composition.[3] "If the social class distribution of the United States were similar to that of top-scoring countries [Korea, Finland, and Canada], the average test score gap [on PISA in 2009] between the United States and these top-scoring countries would be cut in half in reading and by one-third in math," they say. "Because social class inequality is greater in the United States than in any of the countries with which we can reasonably be compared [which in their study also includes Germany, France, and the United Kingdom], the relative performance of U.S. adolescents is better than it appears when countries' national average performance is conventionally compared." Note, however, that even after their adjustment, in math U.S. students still lag behind Canadian, Finnish, Korean, and German students. They do pull even with those in the United Kingdom and come close to those in France, so the United States, in this calculation, remains at best in a three-way tie for fifth out of seven.

Nobody doubts that parental education and child-rearing practices as well as larger cultural and societal influences shape the learning habits that children acquire long before they enter the schoolhouse and play an important role in the development of the human capital of the next generation. We are nevertheless skeptical of claims that performance differences between the United States and other countries can be attributed simply to ethnic heterogeneity or poverty. The United States is not the only country with a diverse population. And as we show in chapters 3 and 4, the proficiency rates of white students and of the most advantaged socioeconomic subgroup of children of college-educated parents in the United States fail to keep pace with the proficiency rates of all students in many countries across the globe.[4]

To us, attempts to exculpate American schools by blaming families or society in general, however popular among those with vested interests in current educational structures and practices, ignore the fact that it is the schools that have been assigned the primary responsibility for educating young people. It is this assignment of responsibility that has driven the dramatic increases in resources that have gone to the public schools and the continuing attention to efforts to improve them.

More important, we know that factors inside the schoolhouse are important for the development of human capital. Researchers have now thoroughly documented what every schoolchild has long known, that the quality of the teacher is enormously important for achievement growth. Good teachers consistently produce more gains in student achievement than ineffective ones.[5] Not only do teachers have large impacts on student test scores, but the quality of the teacher has been shown to have a sizable impact on the probability that a student will go to college and earn more later in life.[6]

The magnitude of teacher impacts on student performance is directly relevant to current discussions. One study, focusing entirely on a disadvantaged group of students in Gary, Indiana, finds that the difference in student performance gains with a highly effective teacher compared to an ineffective teacher was one full year of learning for each academic year: the top teachers produced gains of 1.5 grade levels, while the bottom teachers produced gains of 0.5 grade level in an academic year.[7] Again, these impacts of teachers were recorded for precisely the group of students that are the focus of those emphasizing the centrality of socioeconomic issues. Furthermore, the well-documented differences in teacher effectiveness indicate that three to five years in a class with a top teacher versus an average teacher is sufficient to erase the average achievement gap between poor and better-off children.[8] That is, regardless of the source of any preexisting achievement differences, effective teachers can eliminate them. Family background is not fate.

Just exactly how to improve teacher quality, or precisely what else needs to be done to enhance school effectiveness, is not the subject of this volume. Ideas as to what might be done are plentiful. Merit pay for teachers, limiting teacher tenure, expanded preschool education, holding students accountable through centralized examinations, eliminating the middle school, decentralizing decisionmaking to the schoolhouse, expanding school choice for parents, expanding digital learning systems—all these and other ideas have been placed on the policy table. More and more, the debate over the specific road to take is being informed by quality research. To assess the evidence for each of these and other alternatives would turn this volume from a short book into a massive tome. But we are certainly past saying that there is nothing we can do to educate racial and ethnic minorities and economically disadvantaged students.

We do not know precisely what share of student achievement today is best explained by existing family and societal influences and what share is determined by what happens inside the classroom. But we do know enough to say that schools can make a big difference. One potential reconciliation of the family influence versus schools discussion is that the goal is simply to find the most efficient way to raise the educational performance of U.S. students. It might then make sense to argue that, instead of continuing to put resources into our schools at the current rate, we should divert those funds to income redistribution and social programs.

But even if socioeconomic background were responsible for all of the performance differences with other countries or across our population, we find no evidence that our education problems would go away with enhanced social programs. Substantial analysis suggests that income per se is not the source of education differences.[9] In simplest terms, we may or may not want to pursue a variety of distributional programs or social support policies, but we find no evidence that these would make a significant dent in the education challenges that we face.

Just as important, adjusting the international analysis for social class does not alter the basic fact that this is the population that we have. The real reason for concern about the performance of U.S. students is that international test scores in math say a great deal about the skills that our students will take to the labor force. Our future depends on the skills of our population, and it is time to recognize that we are lagging.

"U.S. Growth Does Not Depend on Student Achievement"

But is it really all that important to boost U.S. student achievement? Does long-term growth in U.S. economic productivity really depend on the quality of the human capital of the next generation? It may be true that economic growth is greater in countries that have higher levels of human capital, as indicated by student achievement, as we show in chapter 2. But is the United States not exempt from the human capital law that ties learning and growth together?

The United States has never done well on international assessments of student achievement. Even during the 1960s, U.S. performance on math and science tests was only about average among the industrialized countries participating in the very first international comparisons of student achievement. Yet the country's GDP growth rate has been higher than the average industrialized country over the past half century. If cognitive skills are so important to economic growth, how can we explain the puzzling case of the United States? Indeed, in figure 2-1, the United States lies above the line, indicating faster growth than would be suggested by its achievement level.

SUBSTANTIVE CONCERNS AND POLITICAL OBSTACLES

Part of the answer is that the economic strength of the United States has come from economic advantages that are quite separate and apart from the quality of its schooling. Overall, the United States has generally less government intrusion in the operation of the economy, including lower tax rates and minimal government production through nationalized industries. The United States maintains generally freer labor and product markets than most countries in the world, there is less government regulation of firms, and trade unions are less powerful than in many other countries. Taken together, these characteristics of the U.S. economy encourage investment, permit the rapid development of new products and activities by firms, reward individuals for invention, and enable U.S. workers to adjust to new opportunities. These features of the U.S. economy are generally viewed as the best economic institutions in the world, something that many other nations are attempting to copy.

It is also the case that, over the twentieth century, the expansion of the U.S. education system outpaced the rest of the world. The United States pushed to open secondary schools to all citizens. Higher education expanded with the development of land-grant universities, the G.I. bill, and direct grants and loans to students. The extraordinary U.S. higher education system is a powerful engine of technological progress and economic growth in the United States not accounted for in our analysis. By most evaluations, U.S. colleges and universities rank at the very top in the world.

Although the strengths of the U.S. economy and its higher education system offer continuing hope for the future, the situation at the K–12 level has an obvious impact on the higher education system as well. The U.S. higher education system will likely be challenged in the near future both by the quality of incoming students and by improvements in higher education across the world.

Other countries are working to secure property rights and open their economies, which will enable them to make better use of their human capital. The historic advantage of the United States in school attainment has come to an end, as half of the OECD countries now exceed the United States in the average number of years of education their citizens receive. Those trends could easily accelerate in the coming decades.

The United States has been able to import skilled immigrants from abroad, often immigrants who have better skills than U.S. workers. These immigrants also increasingly populate U.S. colleges and universities and have frequently been induced to stay in the United States after their postsecondary schooling. The continuation of this pattern will depend directly on both U.S. immigration policies and the nation's ability to offer better opportunities than other countries. Neither is ensured into the future.

In fact, all of our historical advantages over economic competitors—the commitment to universal secondary school attainment, a strong and well-developed economic system, secure property rights and free movement of labor and capital, the world's best universities, and beneficial use of skilled immigrants—are likely to disappear, as many other countries have made great strides in emulating and even surpassing these U.S. strengths. In the future, the United States will have to rely on its skills if it is to sustain its current economic standing. Otherwise, we think that the best projection is that the United States falls back to the growth achievement line in figure 2-1.

The advantages of the U.S. economy will not disappear immediately. But that does not mean that the country cannot benefit from an improved K–12 schooling system. As we demonstrated in chapter 5, the gains that could be expected from improvement are striking. Moreover, these projections, which build on the worldwide experience, may understate the potential advantage of greater human capital to the United States, because the value of added skills is made even greater by its strong political and economic institutions.

SUBSTANTIVE CONCERNS AND POLITICAL OBSTACLES

"There Is a Problem, but the Solution Is More Money"

If the economic benefits from better schools are so great, shouldn't we invest more? That is, put more financial resources into the education system? Won't that turn the tide? That is a very popular view among politicians and the public and, it goes without saying, among school employees. It is a view embedded in the school finance lawsuits, filed in many states, asking for additional financial resources for schools.[10] The lawsuits, which provide a good summary of this idea, do not ask schools to change their operations but instead ask the state to provide additional dollars, which are expected to provide the improved schools that are desired.

But numerous studies show that simply providing more resources gives little assurance that student performance will improve significantly.[11] Some try to find a correlation between education expenditure and student achievement, while others estimate a correlation between class size and student achievement. Neither type of study consistently finds a causal impact on student performance. Results are so consistently negative that a broad scholarly consensus has emerged that simple increases in financial resources or reductions in class size across the board, without more fundamental changes, yield few benefits for student performance.[12]

Of course, perhaps more compelling than the academic debates is the fact that the United States has tried these policies over the past half century with little to no obvious results; the country has dramatically increased expenditures and reduced pupil-teacher ratios, yet NAEP scores of U.S. seventeen-year-olds have been constant.

It is easy to illustrate the issue vividly with our own data. To see whether increased expenditures explain the larger gains in some U.S. states than in others (reported in chapter 6), we plot test score gains against increments in spending between 1990 and

SUBSTANTIVE CONCERNS AND POLITICAL OBSTACLES

Figure 7-1. Relationship between Spending Increases and State Test Score Gains, 1992–2011

Annual test-score gains, 1992–2011[a]

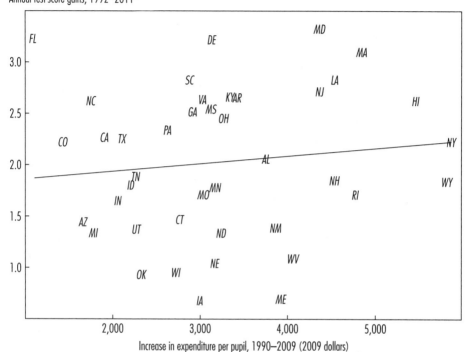

Increase in expenditure per pupil, 1990–2009 (2009 dollars)

Source: Hanushek, Peterson, and Woessmann (2012).
a. Percent of standard deviation.

2009. As can be seen from the scattering of states into all quadrants of figure 7-1, the data offer precious little support for the resource claims.

Just about as many high-spending states showed relatively small gains as showed large ones. Maryland, Massachusetts, and New Jersey enjoyed substantial gains in student performance after committing substantial new fiscal resources. But other states with large spending increments—New York, Wyoming, and West Virginia, for example—had only marginal test score gains to show for all that additional expenditure. And many states, such as Florida and North Carolina, defied the theory by showing gains even when they did not commit much in the way of additional resources. It is true that spending and achievement gains have a slight positive relationship, but the 0.12 correlation between new expenditure and test score gain is of no statistical or substantive significance. On average, an additional $1,000 in per-pupil spending is associated with a trivial annual gain in achievement of 0.1 percent of a standard deviation.

A simplistic view of these findings, convenient as a straw man in public debates, is that money never matters. The research of course does not say that. Nor does it say that money cannot matter. It simply underscores the fact that there has historically been a set of decisions and incentives in schools that have blunted any impacts of added funds, leading to inconsistent outcomes. That is, more spending on schools has not led reliably to substantially better results. How money is spent is much more important than how much is spent.

"The Problem Is Intractable"

That additional money has not had much impact leads some to conclude that nothing much can be done to close the international test score gaps. Such perceptions are reinforced by the utopian nature of education goal setting in the United States. In 1989, for example, the president and the nation's governors announced the goal that all American students should graduate from high school, but two decades later there has been only a small uptick of ninth graders who receive a diploma within four years after entering high school. Further, the governors committed to bring the United States to the number-one ranking in the world in math and science by 2000. As we have seen, that did not happen.

A more realistic set of objectives can be achieved, however, if policymakers are willing to commit to meaningful reforms. If all states could increase their performance at the same rate as the highest-growth states—Maryland, Florida, Delaware, and Massachusetts—the U.S. improvement rate would be lifted by 1.5 percentage points of a standard deviation annually above the current trend line. Since student performance can improve at that rate in some countries and in some states, then in principle such gains can be made more generally. Those gains might seem small, but when viewed over two decades they accumulate enough to bring the United States within the range of the world's leaders— unless, of course, they too continue to improve.

Such progress need not come at the expense of either the lowest-performing or the highest-performing students. In most states, a rising tide has lifted all boats. When states have rapidly improved achievement at the bottom, the high flyers moved ahead as well in almost all of these states.

Let us emphasize once again that we are not recommending here any particular type of reform, though each author has elsewhere provided evidence identifying benefits of specific reforms. What is needed is a commitment to exploring the multiple paths to building a school system that will enhance, not endanger, the long-term prosperity of the country. The real cost to the economy is not the resources needed to put into reform efforts but the losses associated with not improving.

The Central Political Challenge for School Reform

The substantive ideas for reform are plentiful, but the political obstacles to change are no less so. Opposition to change is not the result of intense conflict among the public at large. Differences of opinion do not loom large between parents and nonparents, old and young, affluent and those of more moderate means, renters and homeowners, those from different religious and cultural backgrounds or among groups of varying ethnic background, or even between Democrats and Republicans. By far the deepest cleavage over education policy is between the members of the teaching profession and the general public. One of the authors of this volume, together with his colleagues, learned this after conducting a nationally representative survey of the general public and, separately, a similar survey of public school teachers.[13]

As can be seen in figure 7-2, teachers' opinions differed significantly from those of the general public on seventeen of twenty issues posed in the survey, including the desirability of merit pay, tenure policy, more flexible teacher hiring policies, the desirability of teachers' unions, school vouchers, charter schools, tax credits, annual testing of students, the use of common national standards, the use of tests for grade promotion and high school graduation, tax increases for education, and salary increases for teachers. On eight of these issues, the majority of the public differed significantly from the majority of teachers. No other divisions within the American public were as large or as wide ranging.

The basic opinion divide between the teaching profession and the public is magnified in public discourse by the teachers' unions, which have a stake in representing vigorously the opinions of their members.[14] To survive, union leaders need to fight aggressively on behalf of member interests. In 2010, when a union president in Chicago failed to be sufficiently aggressive, he was replaced by Karen Lewis, who was willing to take the teachers on strike to forestall a variety of school reforms.[15]

In addition to teachers and their representatives, other organizations and institutions in the education sector resist reform. School administrators rise from the ranks of the teaching profession, their salaries and pensions are connected to those of teachers, and they are expected to fight on behalf of the common interests of the sector. Other school personnel—bus drivers, school guards, staff assistants, lunchroom aides, and many more—are often represented by their own unions and serve as valuable political allies when school policy issues arise. School boards, though nominally elected by the public at large, are typically chosen in off-season elections when turnout is small and

SUBSTANTIVE CONCERNS AND POLITICAL OBSTACLES

Figure 7-2. Public and Teacher Support for Selected School Reforms, 2011

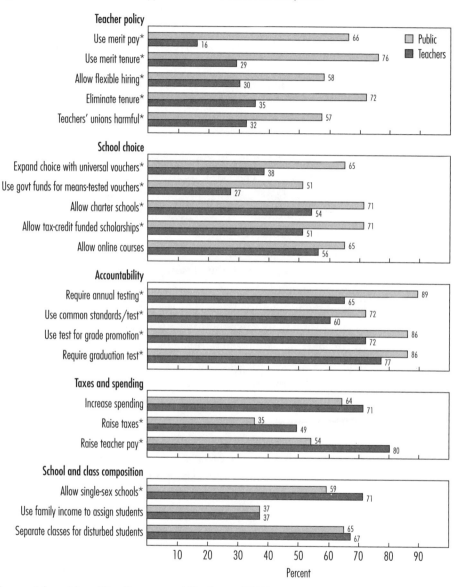

Source: Adapted from West, Peterson, and Henderson (2013).
Note: "Public" does not include teachers. An asterisk (*) indicates that the difference between teachers and the general public is statistically significant at the 0.05 level. Percentages exclude respondents who take neither a positive nor negative position on the issue.

dominated by those who have a stake in the status quo. The safest alternative for a school board member is to defend the status quo.

Education is an industry like any other. Just as the transportation and banking systems have their lobbies, just as farmers organize to protect their interests, just as the real estate industry promotes public subsidies for its sector, so the education industry has a stake in keeping structures as they are while demanding more resources to do its job.

Against a well-organized industry, a poorly informed public has little chance, unless its political leaders understand the crisis the country faces. The public knows that schools are mediocre when viewed from a global perspective.[16] They know that only somewhat more than 70 percent of students graduate from high school within four years after entering ninth grade. Only about one-fifth of the public gives the nation's schools an A or a B on the five-letter scale traditionally used to grade students. But they dramatically underestimate the amount that is spent on schools, leaving them open to claims that the schools can be fixed simply by increasing school expenditure. Also, much of the public thinks the problem lies somewhere other than in their local community; over half say their own local schools deserve one of those two better grades (that is, an A or a B).

Even more important, public discontent with schools is seldom focused on mobilizing the country's political leadership for swift and decisive action. Lofty goals are projected for the distant future, and more money is often promised, but leaders never need to contend with an immediate crisis. There is no fiscal cliff to be faced, no debt limit to be lifted, no bond rating facing adjustment, no trade balance in need of immediate correction. Schools can fail to meet objectives without any short-term calamity. Problem solving can be delayed until next year—or perhaps even the next decade. While the public always places education among the leading issues of the day, the problem never rises to the top of the heap, never becomes the issue to be solved with great urgency, immediately, today.

That is what endangers our prosperity. Only strong bipartisan leadership can spur the kind of action that has propelled schools in the strongly improving countries. Americans could learn by those examples. Or so it seems, if one takes a long-term, global view.

One ray of hope is found in the various state legislatures in which significant change has been shown to be possible. We have seen legislative actions to alter teachers' evaluations, teachers' tenure, teachers' layoff rules, bargaining issues, and more, in a range of states, Wisconsin, Indiana, Florida, Oklahoma, Ohio, Colorado, among them. The fact that these legislatures are willing to make strong statements and to change long-standing laws in these areas suggests that policy might be moving away from the vested interests and more toward improved student outcomes. Extrapolating from these changes leads to a degree of optimism.

A Final Word

Today the United States faces tough political choices related to the long-run fiscal problems of the federal government (and of many state governments). There are agonizing debates about balancing cuts in expenditures against increases in taxes. On top of that, there is increasingly intense debate over the appropriate degree of income redistribution. The most sensational parts of the discussion involve the taxation of millionaires, but the more significant and long-lasting issue involves the growing disparities between those who are well educated and those who are not, a disparity accentuated by the racial and ethnic composition of the two groups.

Each of these issues is much more open to solution if U.S. productivity rates increase. The upward shift in the growth rate of the American economy that would accompany a more highly skilled population can resolve most if not all of the fiscal and distributional problems on the table today. Even more, it would enhance the lives, enjoyment of liberties, and the opportunity for happiness on the part of its citizens.

METHODOLOGY FOR COMPARING U.S. AND INTERNATIONAL PERFORMANCE

This appendix describes the strategy for equating scores across states and nations, first, in terms of proficient and advanced levels of performance (reported in chapters 3 and 4), and, second, in terms of changes in performance over time (reported in chapter 6).

Comparing Proficient and Advanced Levels across States and Countries

For the analyses in chapters 3 and 4, the goal is to compare how students in the different states in the United States are doing with respect to their peers in terms of reaching proficient and advanced levels, respectively. We want to do so with as much detail (by state and social group) as the data permit. To obtain this information, we build a crosswalk between the National Assessment of Educational Progress (NAEP) and the Program for International Student Assessment (PISA), which was administered to representative samples of fifteen-year-old students in sixty-eight of the world's school systems. Note that the sixty-eight school systems include the entirety of sixty-five countries along with three subcountries included in PISA reports: Hong Kong, Macao, and Shanghai. Hong Kong and Macao operated as independent states for a long time and currently have special status.

The crosswalk is developed by looking at the percentage of U.S. students who reach the proficient and advanced levels, respectively, on the NAEP assessment and at the equivalent cut-off score in PISA for that percentage of U.S. students. This gives us the equivalent of the PISA thresholds, allowing us to estimate comparable rates of students performing at the proficient and advanced levels, respectively, for all countries and to compare student performance in each of the states in the United States with that of their international peers.

Our analysis relies on test score information from young adults collected by NAEP in 2007 and PISA in 2009.[1] NAEP is a large, nationally representative assessment of student performance that has been administered periodically since the late 1960s to U.S. students in fourth and eighth grades and at the age of seventeen. Since 2003 it has provided achievement data for students in each of the fifty states in mathematics and reading. PISA is an internationally standardized assessment of student performance in mathematics, science, and reading established by the Organization for Economic Cooperation and Development (OECD). It was administered in 2000, 2003, 2006, and 2009 to representative samples of fifteen-year-olds in all OECD countries as well as in many others.[2]

NAEP is governed by the National Assessment Governing Board (NAGB), which consists of twenty-six educators and other public figures appointed by the U.S. secretary of education. We rely on the 2007 samples of NAEP for eighth-grade public and private school students in each of the fifty states. For each of these jurisdictions, NAEP 2007 calculates the percentage of students who perform at three levels: basic, proficient, and advanced; our analyses in chapters 3 and 4, respectively, use the latter two performance levels.

Our crosswalk from NAEP to PISA aims to identify the relative performance of the class of 2011. NAEP examinations are given to eighth graders, January through March, when most students are thirteen to fourteen years of age. PISA examinations are given to a random sample of students at the age of fifteen, the age at which approximately 70 percent of U.S. students are in tenth grade.[3] To construct the achievement comparisons for the class of 2011, we rely upon the 2007 NAEP test and the 2009 PISA test. In comparing the performance of the class of 2011 on the NAEP and PISA tests at these two different points in time, we assume that no event happened between eighth and tenth grade that significantly altered the performance of American students relative to that of students in other countries.

Because U.S. students took both the NAEP and the PISA, it is possible to find the score on the PISA that is tantamount to scoring at a specific performance level on the NAEP, that is, the score that will yield the same percentage of U.S. students as scored at this level on the NAEP. We describe this crosswalk exercise for the example of performance at the proficient level in math. Given that NAEP identified 32.192 percent of U.S. eighth-grade students as proficient in math, the PISA equivalent is estimated by calculating the minimum score reached by the top-performing 32.192 percent of U.S. students participating in the 2009 PISA test. Using the NAEP and PISA data for the United States as a whole, the crosswalk exercise on the PISA microdata then identifies an estimated PISA score of 530.7 for math proficiency, as defined by NAEP.[4]

With the PISA data, we can obtain an estimate of the percentage of students in all other countries participating in the PISA test above this cutoff, that is, those who reach the level equivalent to the proficient level in eighth-grade math on NAEP 2007. The shares of students who reach the proficient level in eighth-grade math in each U.S. state are taken directly from NAEP 2007. It is assumed that both NAEP and PISA tests randomly select questions from a common universe of mathematics knowledge. Given that assumption, it may be further assumed that students who scored similarly on the two exams will have similar math knowledge, that is, students who scored 530.7 points or better on the PISA test would have been identified as proficient had they taken the NAEP math test. The scaling of PISA straightforwardly reveals that a score of 530.7 points is 31 percent of a standard deviation above the average OECD student score on the PISA, indicating that a similarly accomplished group has been found.

Performing similar crosswalk exercises for reading and for advanced performance, we derive comparable numbers for the other categories as follows. For reading proficiency, 31.223 percent of U.S. students are proficient on the NAEP, which corresponds to a score of 550.4 on PISA. For advanced math, 6.998 percent of U.S. students scored at the advanced level on the NAEP, which corresponds to 623.2 on PISA.

Some of the calculated differences in performance across countries may simply reflect sampling uncertainty or measurement error. We therefore calculate whether the observed differences among states and countries are statistically significant (at the 5 percent level). The requisite standard errors are computed using the methodology described by the OECD.[5] These standard errors account for both sampling uncertainty (including the two-stage sampling design employed by PISA) and test unreliability (as captured by the five plausible values that represent the underlying probability distribution). NAEP 2007 standard errors are obtained from the NAEP website.[6]

Estimating Trends in Performance over Time for States and Countries

For the analyses in chapter 6, the goal is to estimate trends in student performance in the different states in the United States and internationally. To be able to base the trend estimation on as much information as possible, we combine data from as many different tests as possible. Our international trend results are based on twenty-eight administrations of comparable math, science, and reading tests between 1995 and 2009 to jurisdictionally representative samples of students in forty-nine countries. Our state-by-state results come from thirty-six administrations of math, reading, and science tests between 1992 and 2011 to representative samples of students in forty-one of the U.S. states. (Not all U.S. states participated in the state portion of NAEP until 2003.)

These tests are part of four ongoing series: NAEP, administered by the U.S. Department of Education; PISA, administered by the OECD; Trends in International Mathematics and Science Study (TIMSS), administered by the International Association for the Evaluation of Educational Achievement (IEA); and Progress in International Reading Literacy Study (PIRLS), also administered by the IEA.

In the following, we first introduce the international tests and describe our sample of countries. Next, we describe the methodology used to express all international tests on a common scale that is also comparable to the state NAEP performance. Third, we discuss the methodology used to estimate each country's performance trend from the rescaled international test data. Fourth, we describe the procedure used to estimate trends for each U.S. state.

The International Tests and the Sample of Countries

PISA was initiated in 2000 and has been conducted every three years since. Each cycle tests representative samples of fifteen-year-old students in mathematics, science, and reading. As a result, we can use twelve separate PISA tests: three subjects in four waves (2000, 2003, 2006, 2009; for several countries, the 2000 version of the test was administered in 2002, which we consequently use as an observation in the year 2002).[7]

TIMSS has been conducted every four years since 1995. It provides intertemporally comparable measures of fourth- and eighth-grade students in mathematics and science. Given its four testing waves (1995, 1999, 2003, and 2007) administered in two subjects at two grade levels (except that TIMSS did not test fourth graders in 1999), performance information is available for fourteen TIMSS tests.[8] PIRLS was conducted in 2001 and in 2006. It tests the reading performance of fourth graders, providing two tests to be used in the analysis.[9]

In sum, twelve PISA tests, fourteen TIMSS tests, and two PIRLS tests constitute twenty-eight separate test results for those countries that participated in all surveys. Unfortunately, only two countries (Hong Kong and Hungary) participated in all twenty-eight tests. Twenty-seven tests are available for the United States. It did not report the results for the 2006 PISA test in reading, because problems in the administration of the test produced results that were deemed erroneous. The average number of test observations across the forty-nine countries covered in our analysis is just over seventeen (17.2) tests.

We excluded all countries for which results from less than nine separate tests were available and established additional rules for inclusion designed to ensure the trend analyses are based on an adequate number of observations.[10] First, a country's performance on any given test cycle (PISA, fourth-grade TIMSS, eighth-grade TIMSS, and PIRLS) is only considered if the country participated at least twice in the respective cycle, because otherwise no trend information would be contained in that cycle. Second, to ensure that any trend estimate is based on an adequate period of time, a country is excluded if the time span between its first and its last participation in international testing is less than seven years. Third, we do not consider a country if it did not participate after 2006, so as to ensure that all trend estimates extend to recent observations. Together, these rules exclude countries that did not participate in international testing before 2003.

Deriving a Common Scale for All Tests

The international tests are measured on scales that are not directly comparable across the testing cycles. To transform the different international tests to a common scale, we follow procedures similar to those used in prior studies by Eric Hanushek and Ludger Woessmann.[11] The following paragraphs describe the way in which these procedures were applied to the current analysis.

For the estimations reported in figure 6-1, trends over time are based on the 2000 wave of the NAEP testing cycle. Because the scores on the different subjects and grade levels of the NAEP are not directly comparable to one another, we first have to propose a method for making the trends on the NAEP subtests comparable. To do so, we express each testing cycle (of grade by subject) in terms of standard deviations of the U.S. population on the 2000 wave of each testing cycle. That is, within each testing cycle (which is comparable over time), the new scale is such that U.S. performance has a standard deviation of 100 and a mean of 500 in 2000 (the selected mean is arbitrary and without substance for the analysis of trends over time). This is a simple linear transformation of the NAEP scale on each testing cycle.

For example, U.S. performance on the original NAEP score in mathematics in eighth grade is 273.1 (with a standard deviation of 38.1) in 2000 and 282.9 (standard deviation 36.4) in 2009; the 2009 performance is 9.8 points, or 25.8 percent of a 2000 standard deviation above the 2000 performance. By definition, the performance in 2000 on the transformed scale is 500 (standard deviation 100). The performance in 2009 on the transformed scale is 525.8, again 25.8 percent of a 2000 standard deviation above the 2000 performance, now expressed on the transformed scale. Similarly, we can put the 2009 standard deviation on the transformed scale, which is 95.6 (simply, the original 2009 standard deviation expressed relative to the original 2000 standard deviation).

We express each international test on this transformed NAEP scale by performing a simple linear transformation of each international test based on the U.S. performance on the respective test. That is, we adjust both the mean and the standard deviation of each international test so that the U.S. performance on the tests is the same as the U.S. NAEP performance, expressed on the transformed NAEP scale. Specifically, the following steps are taken: First, from the international test expressed on the original international scale, subtract the U.S. mean on that scale. Second, divide by the U.S. standard deviation on that scale. Third, multiply by the U.S. standard deviation on the respective transformed NAEP scale for that year, subject, and grade (interpolated linearly within two available years if year is not a NAEP year).[12] Fourth, add the U.S. mean on the respective transformed NAEP scale for that year, subject, and grade.[13]

Once these steps have been taken, all international tests are expressed on the transformed NAEP scale, where the U.S. population on the international test now has the performance (mean and standard deviation) that it has on the transformed NAEP scale, and all other countries are expressed relative to this U.S. performance on the respective international test. This allows us to estimate trends on the international tests on a common scale, whose property is that, in the year 2000, it has a mean of 500 and a standard deviation of 100 for the United States.

Estimating Trends across Countries

The aim of our analysis is to estimate how each country's performance has changed over time. For that, we use all data points that a country has on the international tests, expressed on the transformed scale. Since a country may have specific strengths or weaknesses in specific subjects, at specific grade levels, or on specific international testing series, our trend estimation holds such differences constant by regressing, for each country, the test scores on a year variable, indicators for the international testing series (PISA, TIMSS, PIRLS), a grade indicator (fourth versus eighth grades), and subject indicators (mathematics, reading, science). This way, only the trends within each of these domains are used to estimate the overall trend of the country. This trend is indicated by the estimated coefficient on the year variable. It represents the annualized change in a country's test performance, expressed as a percentage of the standard deviation of the performance of the U.S. population in 2000.[14]

To see whether the results are affected by the decision to norm all scales on NAEP 2000, we also compared the performance of countries on an alternate scale that is fully independent of NAEP information. We used the TIMSS and PISA tests (and ignored the two PIRLS observations), both of which were performed in 2003, and used the U.S. performance (mean and standard deviation) on both tests in 2003 in order to splice the two series together. PISA scores were left just as they were. Then we rescaled the TIMSS 2003 tests so that the United States has the U.S. mean and standard deviation on the PISA 2003 test (in the respective subject). Then we rescaled the other TIMSS waves so that the U.S. performance (mean and standard deviation) on each is such that its difference from TIMSS 2003 is now measured on the new scale derived from the PISA 2003 comparison. This yields a series in which the TIMSS tests are rescaled in a way that the U.S. performance in 2003 is the same as in PISA and where the TIMSS trends are the original trends but their size is expressed according to the U.S. standard deviation in PISA 2003.

The ranking of the countries remains essentially the same as those reported in the main analysis. On this scale, the U.S. ranks twenty-sixth among the forty-nine countries. However, the annual gain of the United States is only 0.46 percent of a standard deviation, substantially less than the 1.57 percent estimated in the main analysis. Gains for other countries are also substantially reduced in size. In other words, the most reliable information that we report are the gains made relative to those of other jurisdictions, not the absolute size of the gains, which vary depending on the scale that is used.[15] We performed the analysis separately for each subject, for each testing series, and for each grade level, and for mathematics and reading (dropping the science observations). Results are qualitatively similar.[16]

The following procedure was used to estimate the statistical significance of trend lines. Step 1: Calculate the difference between the point estimates of the trends of two countries. Step 2: Calculate the square root of the sum of the variance of the two trend estimates (the standard error of this difference is given by the square root of the sum of the squared standard errors of the two estimates). The result from step 1 divided by the result from step 2 yields the t statistic for the significance of the difference.

Estimating Trends across U.S. States

For the analysis of U.S. states, observations are available for only forty-one states. The remaining states did not participate in NAEP tests until 2003. Annual gains for states are calculated for a nineteen-year period (1992 to 2011), the longest interval that could be observed for the forty-one states.

Trends for each state are estimated using procedures similar to those used to estimate country trends. That is, the NAEP data are first transformed to the common scale that has a mean of 500 and a standard deviation of 100 for the United States population in the year 2000. Then, for each state, the transformed test scores are regressed on a year variable, a grade indicator (fourth versus eighth grades), and subject indicators (mathematics, reading, science). The overall trend of the state is indicated by the estimated coefficient on the year variable.

International comparisons are for a fourteen-year period (1995 to 2009), the longest time span that could be observed with an adequate number of international tests. To facilitate a comparison between the United States as a whole and other nations, the aggregate U.S. trend is estimated from that same fourteen-year period, and each U.S. test is weighted to take into account the specific years that international tests were administered. Because of the difference in length and because international tests are not administered in exactly the same years as the NAEP tests, the results for each state are not perfectly calibrated to the international tests, and each state appears to be doing slightly better internationally than would be the case if the calibration were exact. The differences are marginal, however, and the comparative ranking of states is not affected by this discrepancy.

Table A-1. Country Codes

ARG	Argentina	GER	Germany	NLD	Netherlands
AUS	Australia	GHA	Ghana	NOR	Norway
AUT	Austria	GRC	Greece	NZL	New Zealand
BEL	Belgium	HKG	Hong Kong, China	PER	Peru
BRA	Brazil	IDN	Indonesia	PHL	Philippines
CAN	Canada	IND	India	PRT	Portugal
CHE	Switzerland	IRL	Ireland	ROM	Romania
CHL	Chile	IRN	Iran	SGP	Singapore
CHN	China	ISL	Iceland	SWE	Sweden
COL	Colombia	ISR	Israel	THA	Thailand
CYP	Cyprus	ITA	Italy	TUN	Tunisia
DNK	Denmark	JOR	Jordan	TUR	Turkey
EGY	Egypt	JPN	Japan	TWN	Taiwan
ESP	Spain	KOR	Korea, Republic of		(Chinese Taipei)
FIN	Finland	MAR	Morocco	URY	Uruguay
FRA	France	MEX	Mexico	USA	United States
GBR	United Kingdom	MYS	Malaysia	ZAF	South Africa

TWO MEASURES OF READING PROFICIENCY

The NAEP measure of reading proficiency at eighth grade and PISA's measure of reading proficiency at level 4 are comparable. Here we provide example questions from each.

NAEP

NAEP question at the proficiency level: Consider the coupon in figure B-1. What is an acceptable way to place a $1 Bargain Basement ad in this newspaper?

___1. Phone in the ad, pay by credit card.
___2. Phone in the ad, pay by money order.
___3. Mail the ad, pay by cash.
___4. Mail the ad, pay by check.

If you chose answer 4, you, along with 31 percent of eighth graders, got the question correct.

Figure B-1. Coupon for Placing a Classified Ad in the Bargain Basement

PISA

PISA question at level 4: Underline the sentence in the following story that explains what the Australians did to help decide how to deal with the frozen embryos belonging to a couple killed in the plane crash.[1]

Technology Creates the Need for New Rules

Science has a way of getting ahead of law and ethics. That happened dramatically in 1945 on the destructive side of life, with the atomic bomb, and is now happening on life's creative side with techniques to overcome human infertility.

Most of us rejoiced with the Brown family in England when Louise, the first test-tube baby, was born. And we have marveled at other firsts—most recently the births of healthy babies that had once been embryos frozen to await the proper moment of implantation in the mother-to-be. It is about two such frozen embryos in Australia that a storm of legal and ethical questions has arisen. The embryos were destined to be implanted in Elsa Rios, wife of Mario Rios. A previous embryo implant had been unsuccessful, and the Rioses wanted to have another chance at becoming parents. But before they had a second chance to try, the Rioses perished in an airplane crash.

What was the Australian hospital to do with the frozen embryos? Could they be implanted in someone else? There were numerous volunteers. Were the embryos somehow entitled to the Rioses's substantial estate? Or should the embryos be destroyed? The Rioses, understandably, had made no provision for the embryos' future.

The Australians set up a commission to study the matter. Last week, the commission made its report. The embryos should be thawed, the panel said, because donation of embryos

---

(continued)

to someone else would require the consent of the "producers," and no such consent had been given. The commission also held that the embryos in their present state had no life or rights and thus could be destroyed. Commission members were conscious of treading on slippery legal and ethical grounds. Therefore, they urged that three months be allowed for public opinion to respond to the commission recommendation. Should there be an overwhelming outcry against destroying the embryos, the commission would reconsider.

Couples now enrolling in Sydney's Queen Victoria hospital for in-vitro fertilization programs must specify what should be done with the embryos if something happens to them. This ensures that a situation similar to the Rioses' won't recur. But what of other complex questions? In France, a woman recently had to go to court to be allowed to bear a child from her deceased husband's frozen sperm. How should such a request be handled? What should be done if a surrogate mother breaks her child-bearing contract and refuses to give up the infant she had promised to bear for someone else?

Our society has failed so far to come up with enforceable rules for curbing the destructive potential of atomic power. We are reaping the nightmarish harvest for that failure. The possibilities of misuse of scientists' ability to advance or retard procreation are manifold. Ethical and legal boundaries need to be set before we stray too far.

If you chose the following sentence, you chose correctly: "The Australians set up a commission to study the matter."

NOTES

Notes to Chapter 1

1. PISA is the acronym for the Program for International Student Assessment, which is conducted regularly by the Organization for Economic Cooperation and Development (OECD). The OECD is an association of thirty-four nations, largely the most economically developed in the world, that considers a wide range of economic and social issues.

2. Flattau and others (2006).

3. *Independent Task Force* (2012), p. 8.

4. *Independent Task Force* (2012), p. 3. Emphasis in original.

5. National Commission on Excellence in Education (1983).

6. Peterson (2010).

7. President William Clinton, "Message to the Congress Transmitting the 'Goals 2000: Educate America Act,' " April 21, 1993 (www.gpo.gov/fdsys/pkg/PPP-1993-book1/pdf/PPP-1993-book1-doc-pg477.pdf).

8. President George W. Bush, "President's Letter to the Nation Announcing 'American Competitiveness Initiative,' " February 2, 2006 (http://georgewbushwhitehouse.archives.gov/stateoftheunion/2006/aci/index.html).

9. Subsequent references are to countries, even though some political jurisdictions are not sovereign entities. See figure 4-1 for exact listing.

10. Howell, Peterson, and West (2009); Peterson, Henderson, and West (2013, forthcoming).

11. *Independent Task Force* (2012, p. 29).

12. See http://en.wikipedia.org/wiki/Charles_Brantley_Aycock.

13. Results include those for sixty-five countries and three political subdivisions (Hong Kong, Macao, and Shanghai).

14. U.S. Department of Education (2012, table 195).

15. Peterson (2010, figure 1).

Notes to Chapter 2

1. Murnane (2013).

2. For example, Card (1999); Heckman, Lochner, and Todd (2006).

3. One standard deviation moves a person from the middle of the distribution to the 84th percentile. See the review and discussion in Hanushek (2011).

4. Note, however, that international comparisons are quite limited; see Hanushek and Zhang (2009).

5. Murnane and others (2000).

6. See for example Cunha and Heckman (2007).

7. Additionally, this measure assumes that formal schooling is the primary (or sole) source of education and that variations in non-school factors have a negligible effect on education outcomes. This neglect of cross-country differences in the strength of family, health, and other influences in addition to the quality of schooling is a major drawback of such a quantitative measure of schooling.

8. The initial analysis of Hanushek and Kimko (2000) has now been replicated and expanded in a range of studies, as reviewed by Hanushek and Woessmann (2008), with the most recent addition being Hanushek and Woessmann (2012a).

9. Recent international testing has gone beyond just math and science to include reading. We focus on just math and science for reliability reasons, but including reading performance does not qualitatively change any of the conclusions about international growth differences.

10. There are many technical details involved in the construction of the combined test score measure (see Hanushek and Woessmann, 2012a).

11. Inclusion of initial differences in incomes reflects the fact that it is easier to grow faster when a country starts out behind, because it just has to imitate what more advanced countries are doing instead of inventing new things.

12. Bils and Klenow (2000).

13. Hanushek and Woessmann (2011a).

14. These are more fully reported in Hanushek and Woessmann (2012a).

15. The formal approach is called *instrumental variables.* In order for this to be a valid approach, it must be the case that the institutions are not themselves related to differences in growth other than through their relation with test scores. For a fuller discussion, see Hanushek and Woessmann (2012a).

16. Three potential problems arise in this analysis. First, it just looks at the labor market returns for the individual and not the aggregate impact on the economy of achievement differences. Second, those who migrate at a young enough age to be educated in the United States might differ from those who migrate at later ages. Third, employers may treat people with a foreign education differently from those with a U.S. education. The second two potential problems, however, can only affect the results in complicated ways, because the identification of the impact of cognitive skills is based on a comparison across the home countries. As long as the impact of these is similar for the different origin countries, the results would remain. Any problems would come from different patterns of these factors that are correlated with test scores across countries.

17. Only twelve OECD countries have participated in international tests over a long enough period to provide the possibility of looking at trends in test performance over more than thirty years. The analysis simply considers a bivariate regression of test scores on time for countries with multiple observations. The trends in growth rates are determined in a similar manner: annual growth rates are regressed on a time trend. The plot provides the pattern of slopes in the test regression to slopes in the growth rate regression. Hanushek and Woessmann (2012a) consider more complicated statistical relationships, but the overall results hold. They also hold when the sample of countries is expanded to include the non-OECD countries.

18. It is very unlikely that the changes in growth rates suffer the same reverse causality concerns suggested previously, because a change in growth rate can occur at varying income levels and varying rates of growth.

Notes to Chapter 3

1. Bishop (1992); Murnane, Willett, and Levy (1995). Similarly, it is math skills that are most closely linked to countries' growth performances (Hanushek and Woessmann, 2012a).

2. This overconfidence has persisted over a long period of time; see Lapointe, Mead, and Phillips (1989).

3. NAEP's definitions of the different levels of math achievement are available at http://nces.ed.gov/nationsreportcard/mathematics/achieveall.asp.

4. The question comes from NAEP's online past questions database, http://nces.ed.gov/nationsreportcard/itmrlsx/search.aspx?subject=mathematics.

5. One objection to the question is that the height needs to be ever so slightly larger if it is to encompass balls of that size, but 18.1 cm. was not included among the five response categories.

6. This can be seen from the math performance of U.S. students by level in Fleischman and others (2010).

7. Organization for Economic Cooperation and Development (2009b).

8. A range of sample questions from PISA can be found at: http://nces.ed.gov/surveys/pisa/Items.asp?sub=yes&SectionID=2&CatID=5. This source also provides information on correct scores by U.S. and OECD students.

9. To simplify, we refer to all political jurisdictions as countries, even though a few are not.

10. Our results are qualitatively similar to those reported by the other major international assessment (TIMSS). TIMSS 2007 tested a representative sample of students in Massachusetts and Minnesota. Five countries that had higher average scores than Massachusetts on TIMSS 2007 also took the PISA test. Four of those countries—Taiwan, Korea, Singapore, and Hong Kong—are identified in figure 3-1 as outperforming these states on PISA. Japan also outperformed Massachusetts on TIMSS, but we found Japan's performance to be statistically indistinguishable from that of Massachusetts. Minnesota (whose performance was consistently lower than that of Massachusetts) trailed all five of the above-named countries on both tests, but it outperformed Australia, Sweden, and Norway on TIMSS 2007, even though we identified it as not having done that well. In sum, the Massachusetts and Minnesota performances reported here resem-

ble those reported by TIMSS, though Minnesota students seem to have done modestly better on TIMSS than reported here, while the reverse is true for Massachusetts students (Mullis, Martin, and Foy, 2008, p. 38).

11. NAEP's definitions of levels of reading achievement are available at http://nces.ed.gov/nationsreportcard/reading/achieveall.asp.

12. Organization for Economic Cooperation and Development (2000).

13. For a more detailed discussion of U.S. state standings relative to one another and to peers abroad, see Peterson and others (2011, pp. 11–16).

Notes to Chapter 4

1. "STEM Ed Coalition Objectives" (www.stemedcoalition.org/content/objectives/).

2. Committee on Prospering in the Global Economy of the 21st Century (2005).

3. For example, Lowell, Salzman, and Bernstein (2009) are unpersuaded that there is a crisis in STEM education, suggesting that the larger problem might be on the demand side. They do calculate, however, that a significantly smaller percentage of the most able U.S. high school students entered STEM higher education and subsequent STEM careers over the past two decades than the percentage in the prior two decades.

4. Gates (2007).

5. Hanushek and Woessmann (2012a) extend the analysis of economic growth discussed in chapter 2 to go beyond just average performance. They consider the separate impacts of both performance at the top ("rocket scientists") and performance at the lower end ("education for all"). Their results suggest that both ends of the distribution are important for growth and that doing well at both ends is complementary to growth.

6. Data for the class of 2011. This is only an estimate of parental education, as students tend to overreport parental attainment. In a study of high school sophomores, in which parents reported their own education, 38 percent reported that at least one parent had a college diploma (Education Longitudinal Study of 2002).

7. Loveless (2008).

8. Bandeira de Mello (2011) maps state proficiency levels onto the NAEP scale. In eighth-grade math, a dozen states set their

proficiency level at a point below the NAEP basic level. Only one state, Massachusetts, sets its proficiency level equal to the NAEP proficiency level.

9. Ravitch (2010, p. 109), among others, objects to identifying NCLB effects as early as one year after the law was passed.

10. Loveless (2008) reaches quite different conclusions from an examination of this same information. His findings depend upon his assumption that NCLB was influencing school policy by 2000, two years before the law was enacted. Apart from the problems with this assumption, any conclusions that are sensitive to the choice of one or another year near the cusp are hardly robust; also his analysis extends only to 2007, and high achievers show a growth spurt since that year.

11. Dee and Jacob (2011).

12. Dee and Jacob (2011) find no impact of NCLB on NAEP reading performance.

13. Phillips (2007, 2009). For other studies that compare test score performances across countries, see Hanushek and Woessmann (2011a).

14. Phillips (2007, p. 1). These findings received extensive media attention. As part of its favorable coverage, the *New York Times* quotes Thomas Toch, former codirector of Education Sector: "It shows we're not doing as badly as some say. . . . We're in the top half of the table, and a number of states are outperforming the majority of the nations in the study" (Dillon, 2007).

15. Provasnik, Gonzales, and Miller (2009, p. 3). The report goes on to say, "One reason for this is that the average student performance in developed countries tends to be higher than in developing countries. As a result, the extent to which developing countries participate in an assessment can affect the international average of participating countries as well as the relative position of one country compared with the others."

16. For further reflections on the Phillips studies, see Hanushek, Peterson, and Woessmann (2010, pp. 33–35).

Notes to Chapter 5

1. These simulations follow the development in Hanushek and Woessmann (2011b, 2012b), where the methodology is described in detail. For comparative purposes, these prior simulations in Hanushek and

Woessmann (2011b) look across all of the OECD, and those in Hanushek and Woessmann (2012b) look across European Union countries.

2. The expected work life is assumed to be forty years, which implies that each new cohort of workers is 2.5 percent of the workforce.

3. The path of increased achievement during the reform period is taken as linear. For example, an average improvement of 25 points on PISA is assumed to reflect a gain of 1.25 points a year.

4. As the baseline of the projections, current GDP per capita is based on the 2012 GDP in current dollars from the Bureau of Economic Analysis (advance estimate as of January 30, 2013), projected to 2013 using the real GDP growth forecast from the OECD *Economic Outlook* (of December 4, 2012) and the 2012 population estimate of the United States Census Bureau.

5. According to the most recent data (that refer to 2006), a simple average of male and female life expectancy at birth over all OECD countries is seventy-nine years (Organization for Economic Cooperation and Development, 2009d). Note that these life-expectancy numbers are based on age-specific mortality rates prevalent in 2006 and, as such, do not include the effect of any future decline in age-specific mortality rates. Life expectancy at birth has increased by an average of more than ten years since 1960.

6. This is simply the average annual growth rate of potential GDP per worker of the OECD area over the past two decades (Organization for Economic Cooperation and Development, 2009a).

7. For example, 3 percent is a standard value of the social discount rate used in long-term projections on the sustainability of pension systems. This order of magnitude is also suggested as a practical value for the social discount rate in cost-benefit analysis in derivations from optimal growth rate models (Moore and others, 2004). By contrast, the influential *Stern Review* report that estimates the cost of climate change uses a discount rate of only 1.4 percent (Stern, 2007), thereby giving a much higher value to future costs and benefits, which in our case would lead to substantially higher discounted values of the considered education reforms than reported here. Hanushek and Woessmann (2011b) present projections based on several alternative model parameters, time horizons, and discount rates.

8. The present value of the additional GDP is 6 percent of the present value of GDP over the eighty years. Since about half of the U.S. population is working at any time, it is possible to think of

every worker in the economy receiving greater income of roughly 12 percent on average.

9. The calculation of the cost of the recession reflects the aggregate difference in potential and actual GDP over the period, based on Congressional Budget Office (2013).

10. This goal characterizes NCLB as originally structured. With the advent of waivers to NCLB requirements, most states were released from the obligation to obtain 100 percent proficiency in 2013.

11. The standards for expected achievement in the various states can be compared with those set by NAEP. Only two states—Massachusetts and Missouri—had eighth-grade math proficiency standards in 2009 that were comparable to NAEP's proficiency standards (Peterson and Lastra, 2010). States with the lowest standards include Alabama, Georgia, Illinois, New York, Tennessee, and Virginia. These states set standards below the basic level set by NAEP (Bandeira de Mello, 2011). New York State and Tennessee subsequently raised their standards considerably.

12. The PISA test has a mean of 500 for students in OECD countries, with a standard deviation of 100, implying that we simulate bringing all students up to at least 400 on the PISA math tests. In 2009 the U.S. average on math was 487.

13. For these economic calculations, we rely on an estimated growth model that incorporates the percentage of scores above 600 and the percentage of scores above 400; see Hanushek and Woessmann (2012a). The low-cutoff states refer to authors' calculations for eighth-grade math and rely on the NAEP equivalency in Bandeira de Mello (2011).

Notes to Chapter 6

1. Considerable attention has been given to expanding preschool education. Today about two-thirds of all children between three and five years old attend nursery school or kindergarten.

2. U.S. Department of Education (2011).

3. Peterson (2010, chap. 8).

4. The Progress in International Reading Literacy Study (PIRLS) is the reading assessment conducted by the International Association for the Evaluation of Educational Achievement (IEA).

5. Other, less comprehensive, estimates of trends in student performance across nations include the following: Organization for

Economic Cooperation and Development (2010); Martin, Mullis, and Foy (2008); Mullis and others (2007); Mourshed, Chijioke, and Barber (2010); Organization for Economic Cooperation and Development (2011).

6. After the 2002 federal law, No Child Left Behind, mandated NAEP testing in every state, these nine states participated. Between 2003 and 2011, their annual gains in percent of a standard deviations were as follows: Nevada, 2.94; Montana, 2.06; Vermont, 1.93; Illinois, 1.92; Kansas, 1.43; Washington, 1.30; Alaska, 0.83; South Dakota, 0.81; and Oregon, 0.32. Five of the nine states performed at a level below the national gains during this period, which was 1.85 percent of a standard deviation.

7. The assessment language introduces some confusion. NAEP sets performance standards that it deems proficient, but different (usually lower) definitions of proficiency have been set by the states (see Peterson and Lastra-Anadón, 2010).

8. Bandeira de Mello (2011).

9. Moe (2011).

10. See Hanushek, Peterson, and Woessmann (2012) for details.

11. For the analyses mentioned, see for example Woessmann and others (2009); Mourshed, Chijioke, and Barber (2010); Hanushek and Woessmann (2011a).

Notes to Chapter 7

1. Coleman and others (1966).

2. See www.boldapproach.org/.

3. Carnoy and Rothstein (2013).

4. Other research also suggests that lower levels of student performance in the United States are not due simply to social background factors (American Achieves, 2013). Using data from the 2009 PISA study, America Achieves reports that middle-class students in the United States are trailing their peers abroad. U.S. students were significantly outperformed by peers in twenty-four countries in math.

5. See for example, Hanushek (1971, 1992); Rockoff (2004); Rivkin, Hanushek, and Kain (2005); Chetty, Friedman, and Rockoff (2011); and a number of additional studies reviewed in Hanushek and Rivkin (2010).

6. Hanushek (2011); Chetty, Friedman, and Rockoff (2011).

7. Hanushek (1992).

8. Hanushek (2011).

9. See for example Mayer (1997); Isaacs and Magnuson (2011).

10. Hanushek and Lindseth (2009).

11. The underlying analyses of resources include studies within countries and across countries and have been extensively reviewed elsewhere; see Hanushek (2003); Woessmann (2007); Hanushek and Woessmann (2011a).

12. To view the historical debates, see Burtless (1996) or Greenwald, Hedges, and Laine (1996) and Hanushek (1996). Other controversies on class size are chronicled in Mishel and Rothstein (2002).

13. The specific methodology and the full set of findings are available in West, Henderson, and Peterson (2012) and Peterson, Henderson, and West (2013, forthcoming).

14. See the in-depth analysis in Moe (2011). One measure of the importance of teachers' unions is the general lack of serious analysis about their impacts.

15. For a discussion of the Chicago teachers' strike, see Davey and Yaccino (2012). See also the entry on the Chicago Teachers Union, Wikipedia (http://en.wikipedia.org/wiki/Chicago_Teachers_Union).

16. For public opinion on schools, see West, Henderson, and Peterson (2012) and Peterson, Henderson, and West (2013, forthcoming).

Notes to Appendix A

1. Data for NAEP come from the official website, http://nces.ed.gov/nationsreportcard/. NAEP has also tested periodically a representative sample of students in several other subjects.

2. The OECD, which administers PISA, is an international economic organization encompassing most of the high-income, developed countries of the world. In 2009 it had thirty members; four new members (Chile, Israel, Slovenia, and Estonia) were added in 2010. Sixty-eight countries/economies participated in PISA in 2009 (up from fifty-seven in 2006). Data for PISA 2009 come from the PISA microdata (www.pisa.oecd.org/). PISA assessments build upon earlier international testing; most important are those of the International Association for the Evaluation of Educational Achievement (IEA), now known as Trends in International Mathematics and Science

Study (TIMSS). IEA has conducted assessments since the mid-1960s and is responsible for the TIMSS testing discussed here (www.iea.nl/). Historical PISA scores and those of TIMSS are summarized in Provasnik, Gonzales, and Miller (2009), which also contains references to the original publications for TIMSS.

3. Baldi and others (2007).

4. To cover a broad content area while ensuring that testing time does not become excessive, the tests employ matrix sampling. No student takes the entire test, and scores are aggregated across students. For individual student observations, results are thus estimates of performance obtained by averaging five plausible values, as PISA and NAEP administrators recommend. All PISA calculations use the PISA sampling weights to yield nationally representative estimates.

5. Organization for Economic Cooperation and Development (2009c, chaps. 7 to 9).

6. See http://nces.ed.gov/nationsreportcard/.

7. Organization for Economic Cooperation and Development (2010). The assessment of whether the performance of an individual country on a specific test is deemed comparable over time is taken from table A5.1 in this publication. To this, we have added the math score in 2000/2002, the science score in 2000/2002 and 2003, and remaining matched 2006/2009 scores from the corresponding publications of the respective PISA waves.

8. The TIMSS data are mostly taken from Mullis, Martin, and Foy (2008), which also provides the assessment of intertemporal comparability of individual country performance on a specific test. For countries not participating in TIMSS 2007 but that were in at least two previous cycles, we take the data from the corresponding publications on the respective previous TIMSS trends. As for the TIMSS performance of the United Kingdom, we use the population-weighted mean of England and Scotland, which participate separately in the TIMSS test. To ensure international comparability of tested ages and to avoid testing very young children, TIMSS follows the rule that the average age of children in the grade tested should not be below 9.5 and 13.5 years old, respectively, in grades four and eight; otherwise, the next older grade will be tested in a country.

9. The PIRLS data, including the assessment of country-specific comparability across the two PIRLS waves, are taken from Mullis and others (2007).

10. In fact, with the exception of Argentina, all countries in our analysis have at least ten individual test observations.

11. Hanushek and Woessmann (2008, 2011a, 2012a).

12. To rescale the TIMSS 1995 tests, we use the 1996 U.S. NAEP performance (1998 in reading), which is the earliest available intertemporally comparable NAEP score. For science performance beyond 2005, we use the 2005 U.S. NAEP science performance, which is the latest available, intertemporally comparable NAEP science score. For the rescaling of the PISA tests, we use NAEP tests for eighth graders.

13. Data on U.S. means and standard deviations on the NAEP tests are taken from http://nces.ed.gov/nationsreportcard/naepdata/. Data on U.S. standard deviations on the international tests are taken from the respective publication of each international testing cycle. The U.S. standard deviation on the rescaled 1995 TIMSS performance (which was subsequently expressed on a different, intertemporally comparable scale, without the rescaled U.S. standard deviation being published) was kindly provided by Michael Martin and Pierre Foy from the TIMSS and PIRLS International Study Center at Boston College.

14. Note that, by construction, the international trend estimate for the United States is effectively a weighted average of the U.S. trend in NAEP performance (in the same regression, controlling for grade and subject—math, reading, or science), where the weights are the international test occurrences. These are as follows: 3.6 percent on the fourth-grade math test in 1996 (or 4m96), 3.6 percent on 4m03, 3.6 percent on 4m07, 3.6 percent on 4s96, 2.1 percent on 4s00, 5.0 percent on 4s05, 1.8 percent on 4r00, 1.8 percent on 4r02, 1.8 percent on 4r05, 1.8 percent on 4r07, 4.5 percent on 8m96, 6.3 percent on 8m00, 7.1 percent on 8m03, 1.8 percent on 8m05, 5.4 percent on 8m07, 3.6 percent on 8m09, 4.5 percent on 8s96, 10.5 percent on 8s00, 13.6 percent on 8s05, 1.8 percent on 8r98, 1.8 percent on 8r02, 3.6 percent on 8r03, 1.8 percent on 8r05, 1.8 percent on 8r07, and 3.6 percent on 8r09.

15. Full results are reported in Hanushek, Peterson, and Woessmann (2012, app. B).

16. For results that exclude gains for fourth graders and nine-year-olds, see Hanushek, Peterson, and Woessmann (2012, app. B).

Note to Appendix B

1. Cosgrove and others (2003, p. 50).

REFERENCES

America Achieves. 2013. "Middle Class or Middle of the Pack? What Can We Learn When Benchmarking U.S. Schools against the World's Best?" New York: America Achieves (www.america achieves.org).

Baldi, Stéphane, Ying Jin, Melanie Skemer, Patricia J. Green, and Deborah Herget. 2007. "Highlights from PISA 2006: Performance of U.S. 15-Year-Old Students in Science and Mathematics Literacy in an International Context." NCES 2008-016. National Center for Education Statistics, Department of Education.

Bandeira de Mello, Victor. 2011. "Mapping State Proficiency Standards onto the NAEP Scales: Variation and Change in State Standards for Reading and Mathematics, 2005–2009." NCES 2011-458. National Center for Education Statistics, U.S. Department of Education.

Bils, Mark, and Peter J. Klenow. 2000. "Does Schooling Cause Growth?" *American Economic Review* 90, no. 5: 1160–83.

Bishop, John H. 1992. "The Impact of Academic Competencies on Wages, Unemployment, and Job Performance." *Carnegie-Rochester Conference Series on Public Policy* 37: 127–94.

REFERENCES

Burtless, Gary, ed. 1996. *Does Money Matter? The Effect of School Resources on Student Achievement and Adult Success.* Brookings.

Bush, Jeb. 2013. "Jeb Bush: The Road to Republican Revival." *Wall Street Journal,* March 16.

Card, David. 1999. "The Causal Effect of Education on Earnings." In *Handbook of Labor Economics,* edited by Orley Ashenfelter and David Card. Amsterdam: North-Holland.

Carnoy, Martin, and Richard Rothstein. 2013. "What Do International Tests Really Show about U.S. Student Performance?" Washington: Economic Policy Institute.

Chetty, Raj, John N. Friedman, and Jonah E. Rockoff. 2011. "The Long-Term Impacts of Teachers: Teacher Value-Added and Student Outcomes in Adulthood." NBER WP17699. Cambridge, Mass.: National Bureau of Economic Research.

Clinton, Bill. 1993. "Message to the Congress Transmitting the Goals 2000: Education America Act." *Public Papers of the President* April 21, p. 477.

Coleman, James S., Ernest Q. Campbell, Carol J. Hobson, James McPartland, Alexander M. Mood, Frederic D. Weinfeld, and Robert L. York. 1966. *Equality of Educational Opportunity.* U.S. Government Printing Office.

Committee on Prospering in the Global Economy of the 21st Century. 2005. *Rising above the Gathering Storm: Energizing and Employing America for a Brighter Economic Future.* Washington: National Academies Press.

Congressional Budget Office. 2013. *The Budget and Economic Outlook: Fiscal Years 2013 to 2023.*

Cosgrove, Judith, Nick Sofroniou, Amy Kelly, and Gerry Shiel. 2003. *A Teacher's Guide to the Reading Literacy Achievements of Irish 15-Year-Olds: Outcomes of OECD's Programme for International Student Assessment (PISA).* Dublin: Educational Research Centre.

Cunha, Flavio, and James Heckman. 2007. "The Technology of Skill Formation." *American Economic Review* 97, no. 2: 31–47.

Davey, Monica, and Steven Yaccino. 2012. "Teachers' Leader in Chicago Strike Shows Her Edge." *New York Times,* September 11.

REFERENCES

Dee, Thomas, and Brian Jacob. 2011. "The Impact of No Child Left Behind on Student Achievement." *Journal of Policy Analysis and Management* 30, no. 3: 418–46.

Dillon, Sam. 2007. "Study Compares American Students with Other Countries'." *New York Times,* November 15.

Flattau, Pamela Ebert, Jerome Bracken, Richard Van Atta, Ayeh Bandeh-Ahmadi, Rodolfo de la Cruz, and Kay Sullivan. 2006. *The National Defense Education Act of 1958: Selected Outcomes.* Washington: Institute for Defense Analyses.

Fleischman, Howard L., Paul J. Hopstock, Marisa P. Pelczar, and Brooke E. Shelley. 2010. "Highlights from PISA 2009: Performance of U.S. 15-Year-Old Students in Reading, Mathematics, and Science Literacy in an International Context." NCES 2011-004. National Center for Education Statistics, U.S. Department of Education.

Gates, Bill. 2007. "How to Keep America Competitive." *Washington Post,* February 25.

Greenwald, Rob, Larry V. Hedges, and Richard D. Laine. 1996. "The Effect of School Resources on Student Achievement." *Review of Educational Research* 66, no. 3: 361–96.

Hanushek, Eric A. 1971. "Teacher Characteristics and Gains in Student Achievement: Estimation Using Micro Data." *American Economic Review* 60, no. 2: 280–88.

———. 1992. "The Trade-Off between Child Quantity and Quality." *Journal of Political Economy* 100, no. 1: 84–117.

———. 1996. "A More Complete Picture of School Resource Policies." *Review of Educational Research* 66, no. 3: 397–409.

———. 2003. "The Failure of Input-Based Schooling Policies." *Economic Journal* 113, no. 485: F64–F98.

———. 2011. "The Economic Value of Higher Teacher Quality." *Economics of Education Review* 30, no. 3: 466–79.

Hanushek, Eric A., and Dennis D. Kimko. 2000. "Schooling, Labor Force Quality, and the Growth of Nations." *American Economic Review* 90, no. 5: 1184–208.

Hanushek, Eric A., and Alfred A. Lindseth. 2009. *Schoolhouses, Courthouses, and Statehouses: Solving the Funding-Achievement Puzzle in America's Public Schools.* Princeton University Press.

REFERENCES

Hanushek, Eric A., Paul E. Peterson, and Ludger Woessmann. 2010. "U.S. Math Performance in Global Perspective: How Well Does Each State Do at Producing High-Achieving Students?" Program on Education Policy and Governance, Harvard Kennedy School.

———. 2012. "Achievement Growth: International and U.S. State Trends in Student Achievement." Program on Education Policy and Governance, Harvard Kennedy School.

Hanushek, Eric A., and Steven G. Rivkin. 2010. "Generalizations about Using Value-Added Measures of Teacher Quality." *American Economic Review* 100, no. 2: 267–71.

Hanushek, Eric A., and Ludger Woessmann. 2008. "The Role of Cognitive Skills in Economic Development." *Journal of Economic Literature* 46, no. 3: 607–68.

———. 2011a. "The Economics of International Differences in Educational Achievement." In *Handbook of the Economics of Education*, vol. 3, edited by Eric A. Hanushek, Stephen Machin, and Ludger Woessmann. Amsterdam: North Holland.

———. 2011b. "How Much Do Educational Outcomes Matter in OECD Countries?" *Economic Policy* 26, no. 67: 427–91.

———. 2012a. "Do Better Schools Lead to More Growth? Cognitive Skills, Economic Outcomes, and Causation." *Journal of Economic Growth* 17, no. 4: 267–321.

———. 2012b. "The Economic Benefit of Educational Reform in the European Union." *CESifo Economic Studies* 58, no. 1: 73–109.

Hanushek, Eric A., and Lei Zhang. 2009. "Quality-Consistent Estimates of International Schooling and Skill Gradients." *Journal of Human Capital* 3, no. 2: 107–43.

Heckman, James J., Lance J. Lochner, and Petra E. Todd. 2006. "Earnings Functions, Rates of Return, and Treatment Effects: The Mincer Equation and Beyond." In *Handbook of the Economics of Education*, edited by Eric A. Hanushek and Finis Welch. Amsterdam: North-Holland.

Howell, William G., Paul E. Peterson, and Martin R. West. 2009. "The Persuadable Public: The 2009 Education Next-PEPG Survey." *Education Next* 9, no. 4: 20–29.

Independent Task Force Report on U.S. Education Reform and National Security. 2012. Council on Foreign Relations.

REFERENCES

Isaacs, Julia, and Katherine Magnuson. 2011. "Income and Education as Predictors of School Readiness." Center on Children and Families, Brookings.

Lapointe, Archie E., Nancy A. Mead, and Gary W. Phillips. 1989. *A World of Differences: An International Assessment of Mathematics and Science.* Princeton, N.J.: Educational Testing Service.

Loveless, Tom. 2008. "Part I: Analysis of NAEP Data." In *High-Achieving Students in the Era of No Child Left Behind,* edited by Ann Duffen, Steve Farkas, and Tom Loveless. Washington: Thomas B. Fordham Institute.

Lowell, B. Lindsay, Hal Salzman, and Hamutal Bernstein. 2009. "Steady as She Goes? Three Generations of Students through the Science and Engineering Pipeline." Paper prepared for Annual Meeting of the Association for Public Policy Analysis and Management, Washington, November.

Martin, Michael O., Ina V. S. Mullis, and Pierre Foy. 2008. "TIMSS 2007 International Science Report: Findings from IEA's Trends in International Mathematics and Science Study at the Fourth and Eighth Grades." TIMSS & PIRLS International Study Center, Lynch School of Education, Boston College.

Mayer, Susan E. 1997. *What Money Can't Buy: Family Income and Children's Life Chances.* Harvard University Press.

Mishel, Lawrence, and Richard Rothstein, eds. 2002. *The Class-Size Debate.* Washington: Economic Policy Institute.

Moe, Terry. 2011. *Special Interest: Teachers Unions and America's Public Schools.* Brookings.

Moore, Mark A., Anthony E. Boardman, Aidan R. Vining, David L. Weimer, and David Greenberg. 2004. " 'Just Give Me a Number!' Practical Values for the Social Discount Rate." *Journal of Policy Analysis and Management* 23, no. 4: 689–812.

Mourshed, Mona, Chinezi Chijioke, and Michael Barber. 2010. "How the World's Most Improved School Systems Keep Getting Better." New York: McKinsey and Company.

Mullis, Ina V. S., Michael O. Martin, and Pierre Foy. 2008. "TIMSS 2007 International Mathematics Report: Findings from IEA's Trends in International Mathematics and Science Study at the Fourth and Eighth

REFERENCES

Grades." TIMSS & PIRLS International Study Center, Lynch School of Education, Boston College.

Mullis, Ina V. S., Michael O. Martin, Ann M. Kennedy, and Pierre Foy. 2007. "PIRLS 2006 International Report: IEA's Progress in International Reading Literacy Study in Primary Schools in 40 Countries." TIMSS & PIRLS International Study Center, Lynch School of Education, Boston College.

Murnane, Richard J. 2013. "U.S. High School Graduation Rates: Patterns and Explanations." NBER Working Paper W18701. Cambridge, Mass.: National Bureau of Economic Research.

Murnane, Richard J., John B. Willett, Yves Duhaldeborde, and John H. Tyler. 2000. "How Important Are the Cognitive Skills of Teenagers in Predicting Subsequent Earnings?" *Journal of Policy Analysis and Management* 19, no. 4: 547–68.

Murnane, Richard J., John B. Willett, and Frank Levy. 1995. "The Growing Importance of Cognitive Skills in Wage Determination." *Review of Economics and Statistics* 77, no. 2: 251–66.

National Commission on Excellence in Education. 1983. *A Nation at Risk: The Imperative for Educational Reform.* U.S. Government Printing Office.

Obama, Barack. 2011. "Remarks by the President in the State of the Union Address." Office of the Press Secretary, White House. January 25.

Organization for Economic Cooperation and Development. 2000. "Knowledge and Skills for Life: First Results from PISA 2000." Paris.

———. 2009a. "OECD Economic Outlook." Vol. 2009/1, no. 85. Paris.

———. 2009b. "PISA 2009 Assessment Framework: Key Competencies in Reading, Mathematics, and Science." Paris.

———. 2009c. "PISA Data Analysis Manual." SPSS, 2nd ed. Paris.

———. 2009d. "Society at a Glance 2009: OECD Social Indicators." Paris.

———. 2010. "PISA 2009 Results: Learning Trends—Changes in Student Performance since 2000." Vol. 5. Paris.

———. 2011. "Strong Performers and Successful Reformers in Education: Lessons from PISA for the United States." Paris.

Peterson, Paul E. 2010. *Saving Schools: From Horace Mann to Virtual Learning.* Belknap Press.

REFERENCES

Peterson, Paul E., Michael Henderson, and Martin R. West. 2014 (forthcoming). *Teachers versus the Public*. Brookings.

Peterson, Paul E., and Carlos X. Lastra-Anadón. 2010. "State Standards Rise in Reading, Fall in Math." *Education Next* 10, no. 4: 12–16.

Peterson, Paul E., Ludger Woessmann, Eric A. Hanushek, and Carlos X. Lastra-Anadón. 2011. "Globally Challenged: Are U.S. Students Ready to Compete?" PEPG report. Program on Education Policy and Governance, Harvard University.

Phillips, Gary W. 2007. "Chance Favors the Prepared Mind: Mathematics and Science Indicators for Comparing States." Washington: American Institutes for Research.

———. 2009. "The Second Derivative: International Benchmarks in Mathematics for U.S. States and School Districts." Washington: American Institutes for Research.

Provasnik, Stephan, Patrick Gonzales, and David Miller. 2009. "U.S. Performance across International Assessments of Student Achievement: Special Supplement to the Condition of Education 2009." Washington: National Center for Education Statistics.

Ravitch, Diane. 2010. *The Death and Life of the Great American School System: How Testing and Choice Are Undermining Education*. New York: Basic Books.

Rivkin, Steven G., Eric A. Hanushek, and John F. Kain. 2005. "Teachers, Schools, and Academic Achievement." *Econometrica* 73, no. 2: 417–58.

Rockoff, Jonah E. 2004. "The Impact of Individual Teachers on Student Achievement: Evidence from Panel Data." *American Economic Review* 94, no. 2: 247–52.

Stern, Nicholas. 2007. *The Economics of Climate Change: The Stern Review*. Cambridge University Press.

U.S. Department of Education. 2011. *Digest of Education Statistics, 2010*. National Center for Education Statistics.

———. 2012. *Digest of Education Statistics, 2011*. National Center for Education Statistics.

Vest, Charles. 2009. *Rising above the Gathering Storm: Two Years Later*. Washington: National Academies Press.

West, Martin R., Michael Henderson, and Paul E. Peterson. 2012. "The Education Iron Triangle." *The Forum* 10, no. 1.

REFERENCES

Woessmann, Ludger. 2007. "International Evidence on Expenditure and Class Size: A Review." *Brookings Papers on Education Policy 2006/2007*: 245–72.

Woessmann, Ludger, Elke Luedemann, Gabriela Schuetz, and Martin R. West. 2009. *School Accountability, Autonomy, and Choice around the World*. Cheltenham, U.K.: Edward Elgar.

INDEX